The **Real** Deal *on love and men*

michelle mckinney hammond

Cover by Koechel Peterson & Associates, Inc., Minneapolis, Minnesota

Michelle McKinney Hammond is represented by the literary agency of Alive Communications, Inc., 7680 Goddard Street, Ste #200, Colorado Springs, CO 80920. www.alivecommunications.com.

THE REAL DEAL ON LOVE AND MEN

Published by Harvest House Publishers Eugene, Oregon 97402
www.harvesthousepublishers.com

Library of Congress Cataloging-in-Publication Data
McKinney Hammond, Michelle
The real deal on love and men / Michelle McKinney Hammond.
pages cm
ISBN 978-0-7369-4958-3 (pbk.)
ISBN 978-0-7369-4959-0 (eBook)
1. Man–woman relationships—Religious aspects—Christianity. 2. Love—Religious aspects—Christianity. 3. Men—Psychology. 4. Women—Psychology. I. Title.
BT705.8.M42 2013
241'.6765—dc23

2013012421

Printed in the United States of America

13 14 15 16 17 18 19 20 / BP-KBD / 10 9 8 7 6 5 4 3 2 1

To all those who long to find love that lasts.

To those who just want a real, truthful, and practical dialogue on how to navigate through the curious path of dating, mating, and relating.

To those who have very real questions on matters of the heart.

This book is for you. Hopefully I've answered some of your questions or at least given you enough information to lead you to the answers you need for your love life.

Jesus said, "You will know the truth, and the truth will set you free." Here's to liberating your heart and educating your mind so you can find the love you've been looking for and make the best life choices.

Acknowledgments

Here's to all those who work tirelessly to help make me a better writer, to encourage me to dig deeper, and to remind me to keep it real.

To those who keep asking me questions that spur on meaningful conversations with you, my readers.

To my Harvest House family who continues to support me and encourage me to keep sharing from the Word and from my heart. I couldn't do this without you.

Contents

Time to Get Heart Smart

From the time Adam and Eve got booted out of the Garden of Eden, relationships have been a mystery that men and women have talked about, sung about, ruminated over, and struggled with. Love has often been the elephant in the room—hard to ignore yet tough to conquer. How could something that everyone wants be so hard to find and keep? That is the million-dollar question.

In an effort to find and keep love, I believe we've grown far too polite in our approach. We talk around, over, and under the issue with potential partners. Afraid of stepping on toes and scaring each other away, we fail to ask the questions we should, set the boundaries we need, and have the conversations that are crucial to discerning whether this love is the one we want and deserve. It's time to flip the script on dancing around the issue! Let's have a "down to the nitty-gritty" discussion about what makes love happen and what destroys it. Let's discover how to approach love using our brains while following our hearts.

Over the years I've penned quite a few relationship books, including *What to Do Until Love Finds You*, *Secrets of an Irresistible Woman*, *How to Be Found by the Man You've Been Looking For*, *101 Ways to Get and Keep His Attention*, and *What Women Don't Know and Men Don't Tell You*. You wouldn't believe some of the mail I've received in response. Some people want to share their comments, their thoughts, and their love lives. Some ask questions that make me scratch my head and ask, "Chile, did you read my book?" But I do get it. People read my books and then write to ask questions I've already addressed because they hope I'll give them a different answer. After all, their situations are "special," aren't they? Yeah, right!

Trust me, there are no "special" situations...really. Only our propensity to complicate life and love much more than necessary by trying to write our own scripts rather than follow the laws of the Spirit that hold true whether we like them or not. There are very basic principles that apply to life and love. When we stick to the program and apply the principles to our lives, they will work for us. If we don't, we blow it big time. The bottom line is most people allow their decisions to be based on their emotions instead of making smart choices and then making their emotions line up with that. This creates a huge problem called "disappointment" or, in clearer terms, "heartbreak" because the desired end isn't achieved. Then we want "special" advice and help for what is really a basic problem. Though it might not feel very basic at the time, if we honestly assess our situation, we would have to admit that a basic principle was violated or a clear cue was ignored that led us and our hearts to a place of pain.

Perhaps you were truly innocent and wouldn't have recognized the cues if they'd walked up and slapped you in the face. That is possible. Love is the one vocation in life that no one studies for. We often learn some of our cues from unrealistic movies where people have magical encounters and passionate love affairs without any of the work needed to secure love in real life or any of the consequences of violating God's principles when the music stops playing.

Unfortunately, you probably do have to know a few things your mama might not have told you about to get the love you want and need. Though you must include spiritual principles in your love repertoire, love can't be solely spiritualized. A balance of pragmatism and practicality must be blended with the spiritual side to get the best outcome in every area of your life. In other words, don't just follow your heart. You need to also listen to the Holy Spirit and use your head.

So here are my "tell the truth and shame the devil" answers to many of the questions I've fielded over the years. Hopefully the information will help you navigate your search for love with better results than what you've been getting. No one likes the taste of medicine, but when you take it you get well. So stop nursing and rehearsing unhealthy habits that keep you in a state of flux about love. It's time to get heart smart and love wise once and for all.

What's the real deal on love and men? Dig in, my friend. I'm not afraid to tell the truth, and the truth has been known to set sisters free!

1

The Power of One

"I'm *lonely...so lonely I don't need to peel an onion to cry.*" This is a line from a poem I wrote many years ago. Looking back, I think, "How pitiful is that?" What could have made me plummet to the depths of writing something so morose? It came from a place of deep disappointment that once again I'd found myself at the end of yet another failed relationship. The future looked bleak. I couldn't see a positive today, much less tomorrow. I was alone and unloved. Neither state was the truth, but that was how I *felt* in the moment. Unfortunately, I allowed those untruths to consume me. The emptiness was excruciating.

Loneliness is a sad affair, and that's the gospel truth. But ask me why. *"Why, Michelle? Why is life this way?"* It's not! No one has to be lonely. Loneliness is a mess we create. Now, being alone and being lonely are two different things, and it's important to know the difference. Why? Because loneliness can chase you into a desperate place where you make choices that aren't good for you, your heart, or anything that has to do with your health.

Single people aren't the only ones who get lonely. Married people get lonely too—just listen to some of your married friends. Having the title "married" doesn't guarantee wonderful feelings of being loved or marvelous togetherness all the time. We have a high divorce rate to confirm that marriage is not the utopia many a love-starved single wants to believe it to be. If you're by yourself and feeling sorry for yourself, you need to conquer the "lonely" beast.

This monster will invite you to his self-pity party, sit you down, and feed you all kinds of lies packed with "why me" fillings and topped with "poor me" sauces that will make you sick and silly. You can blame your dread of being alone on the media if you like. After all, everyone on TV and in the movies eventually has somebody. But the truth of the matter is you can't believe the hype. Remember, those worlds are make believe! Unfortunately, the media and popular culture try to convince us we're abnormal if we're by ourselves or not running through fields of clover with the ones we love. Argh!

Let me eliminate some of your misery by breaking down a few myths. First, "alone" is not a negative state of being. Alone can be a great place. When Adam was strolling around the garden with God, he was so caught up in the wonderfulness of that experience that it probably never occurred to him that he was the only one of his kind.

Alone can be a place of empowerment where you take stock of your world and your gifts, and then use that knowledge to master your personal universe and exercise the options available to you without delay or interruption. This is an opportunity to become a better you—for God, for yourself, and for whomever you choose to share yourself with.

Alone can also be a great time to enjoy special delights. I don't know about you, but shopping is sacred to me. I want to be alone for that activity. I don't need input from the peanut gallery on what to buy or not buy. I can shop 'til I drop all by myself! I also love a good hot bubble bath. Just me, candles, music, and lots of suds. Ah, heaven...

Alone affords you the solace to focus and get clear on issues in your life. You know, plan your work and work your plan. It can be a place of deep healing if you're not afraid to listen to the silence, to God, to yourself, and to whomever else God brings to mind when you're alone.

I've found that people who have a hard time being alone often have a difficult time being with people too. The bottom line is your relationships with others will only be as healthy as the relationship you have with God and yourself when you're flying solo. Quiet as it's kept, a lot of folk don't like being alone because they don't want to be quiet enough to hear truths that can only be heard in the silence. They prefer to fill their world with ambient noise to drown out the voices of God, reason, and other inputs that might challenge them to lift the bar when it comes to their lifestyles and habits. For people who know they need to deal with some things about themselves they've been ignoring on purpose, a place called alone can be excruciating.

If you don't master a solo act, your duet is going to be a hot mess. You will either rely on the other person to complete you or at least fill in all the blanks in your world. Let me tell you right now, baby girl, that no man on the face of this earth can do God's job. If you're looking for someone to complete you or fill your voids, both expectations will lead to the same sad end—abandonment when the men cave under the pressure of your neediness or your disappointment that they don't fill the bill you give them. So what's a girl to do? How do you get past the place called lonely? By getting past yourself.

> Loneliness has nothing to do with the number of people in a room. It has everything to do with how you look at life.

Um hmm. You see the major malady of most human beings is something called self-involvement. We tend to spend most of our time gazing at our own belly buttons. The more we look at ourselves, the more everything that is missing or wrong with us is magnified. Things that are temporary appear permanent, which creates a state of hopelessness. Hopelessness tends to make us think, talk, and act crazy. Everything is based on how we *feel* in the moment. That's when we think or write letters like this one.

Dear Michelle,

I have to confess that I bought your book Sassy, Single,

and Satisfied, but I haven't read it yet because, to be perfectly honest, I don't want to be single and satisfied. I want to be married with children.

I don't know what's wrong with me. I am so miserable I can't stand myself. I don't go anywhere or do anything because I hate the way I look and feel. No one talks to me. There's a guy I like at my job, but he doesn't even look at me. My mother says I'm suffering from depression. Maybe she's right. So can you give me the crib notes on how to be sassy and satisfied even when you're single? I don't think I have the strength to read your book.

Miserable, Bored, and Getting Fat

Dear MBGF,

I have felt like you do. However, you've got to snap out of it! Trust me, I'm not being mean when I say that. Here's the ticket. You have a choice. You have to decide how you're going to look at life—and then line up your actions accordingly. Your emotions will catch up with you once you get busy about the business of creating the life you want.

I tell people who complain about being bored that they are bored because they are boring. No one is going to make life happen for you, girlfriend. Let me guess your schedule. You go to work, you go to church (perhaps), you go home. This is your routine 24/7. Right? It's time to flip the script! Get out there and get a life! You've got to turn your life into a party that people want to attend. No wonder that guy at work isn't talking to you if you're walking around looking sad and gaining weight. Would you want him if he were doing that?

You're the only person who can change your life. That is the power of one. Now is the time to set the standard you want *your future partner to line up to. You can't hand someone a blank piece of paper and expect him to come up with the script you want to hear. That's too much work and unrealistic. Why not make it easy for him? Get the life you want, and then allow those you're interested in to join in and be part of what you've already begun.*

Let me ask you a question. How would you end the sentence, "I've always wanted to...?" Why not do that thing now? Take that class. Go to that country. Do the activity. Get started! Take the first step! Once you get going, guess what will happen? You'll meet other people with similar interests, and that will lead to somewhere more exciting than where you already are. Remember, nothing plus nothing equals nothing. So start something that puts a light in your eyes, a pep in your step, and excitement in your voice. Get sassy and you'll become a walking invitation for love.

Loneliness has nothing to do with the number of people in a room. It has everything to do with how you look at life. You are in control of your personal world and space. Create the life you want for yourself by embracing the life God has given you! He has promised you a life more abundant than the one you had before you knew Jesus Christ. Accept it, live in it, enjoy it!

Love always (even when no one else is watching).

Michelle

Keeping It Real

Too many people sit on the sidelines waiting for someone else to make their lives happen. Life happens when *you* make it happen. Love happens when your lifestyle makes you interesting and lovable because of what *you* bring to the party. If you're bored, the person who could make life interesting for you isn't going to stop to entertain you because he is looking for someone who is as interesting as he is! We attract what we are and what we think we deserve. That can be good; that can be bad. Take the "I's" out of loneliness and you're left with "one-i-ness." Look past yourself and start giving away the love you already have—for others and for life.

Let me put it on the line: Get over yourself. Life is bigger than you. Love is not just about what you get out of it. It's about what you're willing to give to others...and not just to someone you might be interested in loving. Get involved with everyone God makes available in your world right now—keeping it healthy, of course.

Too many people are lonely because they insist on deciding where love will come from. You pray for love to come your way, but then you swat away many potential sources. One of the great surprises about love is it usually comes wrapped in packages you may not expect. Part of the fun of life is living spontaneously, embracing variety, and being open to risks. The more love you generate, whether it be to children, old folks, strangers on the street, or even pets, the more you will attract because you will be surrounded by love chemistry.

I believe we give off a "scent of love," invisible pheromones that signal to the world we are loving. Desperation and loneliness give off scents too—odors that repel the very thing you long for. So give love freely to everyone around you 'cause it's free. You will *always* get a return from your investment. Love is yours to give away or keep, but keeping it isn't any fun. Love begins and ends with you...and so does loneliness. You determine which one you'll embrace. So get rid of the lonely and get a life that is full of fun, joy, and fulfillment.

Love begins with you celebrating life by realizing at the center of your world stands the "Lover of Your Soul"—the One who created love, the One who loves you more than anyone else ever can and ever will, the One who created you. Knowing you're loved by the ultimate Lover should put a smile on your face and a pep in your step. Ever notice how the minute someone is interested in you all the others swarm around you too, just like bees drawn to honey? Yeah, girl, you need to get that "I am loved already" look—your own personal feel-good vibe. Ramp up your life. As my girl Luci Swindoll says, "Don't just be interested, be interesting!"

Loneliness is really the fruit of selfishness, so you know what that means: You need to become interested in someone or something other than you! Something not attached to your desires, neediness, or expectation to get something back. Give yourself to something that needs your time and attention and watch what surprises will happen. Life doesn't have to be lonely after all. And it will only be as lonely as you allow it to be.

2

Me, Myself, and...

In one of my favorite musicals, *West Side Story*, the heroine sings that she feels pretty. So pretty, in fact, that she pities any girl who isn't her. She goes on to say she feels charming, stunning, entrancing, and so forth. It seems a little audacious on her part, perhaps, but it does bring up an important truth. Have you ever been attracted to someone with low self-esteem? C'mon now, admit the truth. If someone can't like himself, that's usually enough to convince you not to either, isn't it? After all, who knows him better than he does (besides God)? Perhaps he knows why you should or shouldn't like him. Hmmm...when guys tell you, "You're too good for me," believe them.

But what about you? People attract what they are and who they believe they deserve. And the two trains of thought are not that exclusive from one another. If you are what you attract, what have you been attracting or not attracting? What do you believe you deserve, and what have you been settling for? The sword cuts both ways.

At the beginning of any healthy relationship or interaction is you. You're the central character in your love story. A lot rests on how you see yourself. If you don't like you, it's going to be very hard for you to have genuine, positive feelings for anyone else. Or worse still, you won't be able to handle or receive true love if someone came up and offered it to you. Small wonder then, that right up there after the commandment to love God with all your heart, soul, mind, and strength is the command to love your neighbor *as you love yourself* (Mark 12:31-33). Jesus is not talking about being an egomaniac or being full of yourself. He's talking about having a healthy appreciation and respect for God's creation. That includes you and everyone else you encounter. Since you will always be your first human reference to everything, how you take care of yourself is going to naturally be reflected in how you deal with people around you.

It's quite easy to see that critical people are also hard on themselves, while people who don't take themselves that seriously usually have an abundant measure of grace for others. To the pure, everything is pure. Crooks don't trust anyone, and they usually recognize one another. Often what irritates us in others is what we're most guilty of ourselves. This is why we tend to recognize that quality so quickly. So go ahead—say ouch and get over it.

What does it mean to love your neighbor as you love yourself? Are you kind to yourself? Do you forgive yourself when you mess up? Do you celebrate when you accomplish something? Do you speak the truth to yourself in love? If you do, you will exercise the same grace with others. If you don't, you've got some major work to do on yourself. Perhaps you were raised by a parent who was critical or called you ugly or stupid or worthless. Unfortunately, these things may have stuck in your spirit and taken root. In the mind of children, what parents say is always considered right. And those early impressions from others often lay the foundation for beliefs that affect our mindsets and influence our ability to give and receive love for the rest of our lives.

Perhaps you need to make friends with yourself. Perhaps you need to educate yourself about you. Find the things that should be celebrated and change the things you've simply tolerated and wished you would change. *You have the power to change your world and your view of you.* People will see you through the lenses you're looking through. And that can take you on a road that leads to nowhere but disappointment if you have a negative view of yourself and reinforce that view to others.

What are your fears about love? I confess that for a long time I was attracted to men who wouldn't commit to relationships because I was a commitment phobe. I was afraid of love so I felt safe with men I knew wouldn't commit because I'd never be forced to do the same. Yet deep within I longed for the very commitment I was running from. Many people are divided internally like that. Their minds say one thing but their hearts say another. Usually it takes getting sick and tired of being sick and tired to force people to look in the mirror and make the mental shift. Can you relate? If so, you have to decide and acknowledge what you truly want and then be willing to do whatever you have to do to get it. This is where your work needs to begin. Get rid of the lies that rob you of the love you want, the love you deserve (and you do deserve it because God created you!).

Go ahead and stand in front of a mirror to take stock physically, emotionally, spiritually, intellectually, and professionally. Make a list of the things you can celebrate about yourself. Make a note of the things others celebrate about you. Do your lists match? Perhaps you have trouble receiving a compliment. Why is that? What lie blocks the truth of who you really are and robs you of the joy you should be free to experience when you've done something positive or someone recognizes something positive in you? Yes, it's time to dismantle the lies and false beliefs that have made you a person who sabotages your opportunities for love.

No One New Ever Comes Along

Did you say you never meet anybody? That just isn't true. You have the potential to meet someone new every day. But based on how you feel about yourself, perhaps you're unconsciously repelling people. The Bible says that to make friends you should show people you are friendly. Proverbs 22:11 says, "One who loves a pure heart and who speaks with grace will have the king for a friend." People would like to meet you, but maybe the frown on your face told them not to bother speaking to you. Maybe you're not even aware that your face, demeanor, posture, and attitude are sending signals that thwart possible friend and love interests. Trust me, people are checking you out. Whether these are people you're interested in is another story, but they are around you all the time. The bottom line is that most people are unaware of a lot of what is going on around them. Lack of knowledge can cause us to draw unhealthy conclusions, including "no one is interested in me" and "no one cares." Perhaps the disinterested party is really you...or the vibes you're sending out.

If how you feel about you is often how others will feel about you, then it's time to check yourself and do the work it takes to make an attitude shift. Renew your mind. Find out what God thinks about you and embrace His healthier thoughts about who you are. You are a most incredible creation because you are *His handiwork*! And everything He makes is good! Say that to yourself until it takes root in your spirit so you believe it without question or hesitation. You have to change your confession if your self-talk is negative.

I have a friend who always gives the same response when I ask "How are you?" No matter what is going on, he answers, "Fantastic!" And you know what? No matter what is going on with him, things usually take a turn upward. He refuses to be ruled by emotions or circumstances. He will not bow to feelings of failure or any negativity he's tempted to feel when facing difficulties.

If you're not feeling upbeat and positive, you need to decide to take the steps that will make your emotions line up with the way *you choose* to view your world (tempered with reality, of course). So often if we look the part and act the part, our emotions and attitudes will eventually line up. If you carry yourself as a person who should be taken seriously when it comes to love (or a job interview or something else you're pursuing), others will respond to you in kind. The more positive responses you

So often if we look the part and act the part, our emotions and attitudes will eventually line up.

receive, the more your mindset will change because the new ideas and feelings are being confirmed instead of the old ones.

For the most part, if you and I really 'fessed up and kept it real, we'd acknowledge that in most instances we are our own worst enemies. We get what we allow—nothing more, nothing less.

Dear Michelle,

I seem to be a magnet for deceit, manipulation, and dishonesty. I'm told we reflect or attract what's inside of us. People get to know me, are turned off, and run. I generally try to live honestly and lovingly and to always think about how God would like me to behave. I am a good woman, mother, and all-around person, but I keep coming up short in the love department (men, friends, family). I am not the worst person in the world. I don't seek to hurt others. I'm not perfect, but I generally seek to do good and see good in others. But for some reason people are turned off when they meet me. On this vast green earth, does God truly not have one person willing to stand by my side? Am I that unattractive? Am I that "boring" as you might say? I seem to repel others, so I'm left alone to raise my children.

Sincerely,
Major Turn Off

Dear MTO,

Of course God has someone who will be willing to stand by your side, but you have to believe that and act accordingly. Your letter is laden with conflict. On one hand, you seem to have a positive picture of yourself; on the other hand, you don't. Being "a bad magnet, a turnoff, a repellant"—those are pretty strong descriptions! Is that how life really is? Everybody believes you are terrible or are turned off by you?

When you are the common denominator in all the situations you've listed, you must stop and ask yourself some very deep questions. First, is it really you or is it them? Do all those people know one another? If not, that rules out the theory that they all got together and conspired to ruin your world. Therefore, you need to ask if there is something you need to change. Perhaps your choice of friends, men, and associates? Perhaps a personal habit that could be putting a damper on your relationships? Don't be afraid to ask the people you interact with questions to see if their answers sound like a scratched CD. If they do, you need to listen to the song and see if you can fix the scratch or change the words. Sometimes the truth hurts, but it's always good medicine if it will help set you free from whatever negative cycle is going on.

If you're making wrong choices of who to walk with or not exercising enough discernment on who to trust, keep, or eliminate, the onus falls on you to master your personal world. Take charge! Decide what you want your relationships to look like and then find people who fit that healthy picture. Begin by being that picture yourself—from the inside out. If you believe you deserve kindness in your life, cruelty and neglect will be unattractive to you, so you'll be better able to recognize it in another person's character right away. A huge part of stopping the madness in life is cutting it off before it starts, girlfriend. Ask God to expose the hearts of the people around you before you invest yours. Why? Because this knowledge is priceless and you'd better know it.

Trusting in God with you,
Michelle

Okay, I couldn't resist sharing one more similar story. Same root, different fruit.

Dear Michelle,

My ex-boyfriend and I broke up more than 3 months ago. We'd been together for around 5 years. It was an on-and-off relationship. There were many problems in the relationship, including him not giving me enough time and not being thoughtful. On my part, I was easily angered, strict, and a little bit of trying to force God into him. We are both Christians, but he's not truly committed to God. He doesn't enjoy going to church or reading the Bible.

Two weeks after the last breakup, he promised me we would try again on his birthday, which was September 28. On that day, I reminded him of his promise. Although he agreed to try things out, his resentment was apparent. He said he was really being forced to do it. I hadn't contacted him for the 3 months in-between because I was really looking forward to fixing things with him. When I greeted him yesterday for his birthday and sensed his resentment, I started crying again. The feeling of rejection was overwhelming.

I really hope that we can still work things out. I am so lost and confused. I want to be with him so much, but I feel that it's wrong to run after him. How can I show him that I am better now if he won't give me a chance? Please help me!

Sincerely,
Trying to Make It Work

Dear TMW,

You said you didn't want to pursue him, but you are. Why are you reminding him he's supposed to give you another try? My even greater question to you is why are you trying to make it work? You said he didn't give you enough time. He wasn't thoughtful. He wasn't committed to God. Basically he didn't do anything that was important to you. Furthermore, you stated he resented being reminded he was supposed to give you another try again on his birthday. (On his birthday! How convenient—just in time for you to buy him a present, right?)

You say he inspires in you feelings of deep rejection, being lost, and confused. Why, why, why do you want to be with this man? While you are trying to be worthy of him, he is not worthy of you. Is this all you think you deserve? Girl, this guy is not God's best for you. The guy doesn't fit God's love design for women who belong to Him.

First of all, the man is supposed to be pursuing you. He is supposed to think you are the best thing since sliced bread so he'll want to do whatever it takes to win your love. You need to get a revelation of your worth. You were created by God! He knew you before you were born and has plans for you (Psalm 139; Jeremiah 29:11-13). He loves you and died for you (John 3:16).

This man you're chasing isn't God's best for you. I say drop him like you would a hot potato and move on. Allow yourself to be found by someone who loves God and you, in that order, without the drama and heartache. You deserve better. Okay, here's the deal. You won't put up with nonsense like him if you believe you deserve better. You need to kick boyfriend to the curb, and then work on yourself until you have a better appreciation of your value. While you're at it, pick up a few of my books to help you get your head and your heart together. They're listed in the back of this one, and each book is packed with affirmations on who you are in Jesus and how much you deserve to be loved. Trust me, when you tighten your perception of yourself and your worth, you'll flip the script on your expectations. Men like the guy you've been with won't be attractive to you once you realize you deserve someone who doesn't need to be schooled about God or how to love a woman He created.

I know this is probably hard to hear, but come on now! God

3

Get a Life

Let's get the right perspective straightaway. The marriage altar is not a destination. It is a gate you pass through on the way to the rest of your life with a partner. In other words, keep it moving, sister! Don't get stuck putting your life on hold. Don't wait for someone else to come and make your life happen. Create a life that someone else will want to join you in, one that will attract someone in whose life you'd like to join. This means getting over yourself, looking up to see all that life has to offer, finding all the people you get to be a blessing to, and getting on with the business of living.

I've got to reach back and pull a page from the book of Ruth on this one. (The famous Ruth of the Bible, that is.) After the death of her husband, Ruth moved to a foreign place where she didn't know anybody but her mother-in-law. Yes, Ruth ended up marrying a rich man, but that was not her intent. She didn't go looking for a husband. I'm sure that was the last thing on her mind. As a matter of fact, where she was going her people, the Moabites, were considered pagans, so her marriage prospects were slim to none. She went to the land of Judah with a completely different agenda, one that had nothing to do with husband hunting. In fact, Naomi had been concerned about whether

Ruth could find a new husband in Judah. But Ruth decided to stick with Naomi so she could take care of the elderly woman she loved.

On that note and once in Judah, Ruth went out to the fields to see what she could glean for their sustenance. Her steps took her to the fields of an eligible man who noticed her immediately because she was different. She wasn't trying to catch his eye. She was there handling her business, collecting the leftovers from the crops. I'm sure she didn't go with makeup on, locks flowing, or fancy attire. No, no, no. She didn't go to flirt; she went to work. And she *still* got her man. As a matter of fact, brother man was so impressed with the fact that she was all about being resourceful, taking good care of her mother-in-law, and getting on with her life he felt compelled to help her, protect her, provide for her, and marry her!

Are you getting the principle here? Get on with your life. You never know who is watching. And if they are watching, they will be impressed by what they see.

I find it interesting that Ruth's sister-in-law, Orpah, upon hearing there would be no potential love connections in the land of Judah, decided to go back home. We never hear anything else about her. Did she find another love? We are never told. The rest of her story wasn't included—my guess is because her personal quest made no contribution to the kingdom of God. Such is the life of those whose only goal is to get a man and do nothing else that contributes to God's greater plan. They don't do anything worth writing home about.

Back to the crux of this issue. I hear you, ladies, when you ask *where are the men*? The men are busy doing what they do, and you should be too. Most men don't make getting married a primary mission in life. They're focused on the activities that define their masculinity which, by the way, are the things that make them attractive to us. Things like establishing themselves, getting a job, excelling in their profession, and making money. You know, that whole mandate Adam got in the garden: have dominion, be productive (fruitful), and multiply.

So how do you meet these men who have something to offer? It is true that it's harder to meet people once you exit stage left from high school and college. In school there were all sorts of clubs and forums that made meeting lots of new people easy. At that point in time, there were plenty of eligible folk to choose from. The possibilities were endless. So if you didn't grab your potential mate while you were in school, once you graduated and got on with the business of making a life for yourself, you discovered something not so exciting. The pool of eligible males seemed to dwindle to a tired little trickle. Uh huh. You settled into the routine of going to work (it's not wise to mess with people at work), going to church (if you do that), and going home. Generally speaking, your extracurricular activities were not so extra any more. Gone were the clubs, athletic games, functions, and dances to attend. And you realized you might have passed up your easiest chances of capturing someone's attention.

Then there are those who wasted a lot of time looking for love in all the wrong places and making several bad choices. Now you look into the mirror and realize you're older and still unattached. Or perhaps you opted for career first and family second. Again you find yourself alone. Where are the men now that you've arrived and have something to offer? You missed the first wave, sistah. After 31, you've pretty much found that most men have gotten married while you were being myopic about your life.

Yes, it is possible to have a love life while building a life. As a matter of fact, my Bible tells me that two are better than one because then you have some help. Can I get an "Amen!" for some help? I think all this independence nonsense has been overblown and created by a bunch of selfish, depressed people. Now that you're in line for the next wave of men, you've got mostly the divorced and widowed. Be honest, when you meet a man who is over 35 you usually wonder why he isn't married, don't you? Is he a player? Is he gay? Is he selfish or indecisive? What is he? Just remember, the longer you delay finding a mate, the more baggage both of you will have to unpack. Now, I do realize that for some people God's timing wasn't for you to marry when you were young. But I also know that some folks just made not-so-great choices for pretty crazy reasons and are dealing with the consequences.

However, there is hope for your love life! God is able to redeem the time, but now a little more effort and cooperating with Him are required on your part. First things first. Rediscover your old interests that you've retired and also find new ones. That's right! Get out of the house. Circulate. Meet people active in arenas that interest you. This will help you run into people who have the same interests as you do. That's a good place to start. How can two walk together unless they agree, right?

There is hope for your love life! God is able to redeem the time, but now a little more effort and cooperating with Him are required on your part.

Next, find people to invest yourself in. When you give love away, it often comes back to you from unexpected places. That lady at the old folks home might have a delightful son. That afterschool program you're helping out at might be where you meet a sweet single dad. That night out at the theater might put you in position to meet someone else who loves the arts. You never know, but you won't find out until you get out there. The thin line that must be mastered with this exercise is focusing on doing life for enjoyment. A man who loves you will be the cherry on the cake of your life—not the cake itself. Be authentic in your pursuit of life, and allow love to find you doing your thing.

Love who is available to be loved in your world right now, right where you are. Love begets love. Just because you don't have a special man at this minute doesn't mean you can't have a love life. You need to be walking around "in" love and feeling loved already. Stir up those love pheromones, girl. It's called chemistry. Ever notice the minute someone expresses an interest in you other brothers start coming out of the woodwork? Uh huh, those are probably pheromones at work. Something is activated when we get excited about love. It puts a flush on our cheeks, a light in our eyes, a smile on our lips, and a pep in our step that makes us downright attractive. Like I said, love attracts love. So if you don't have a man, exactly who are you to be in love with? Pull those lips back in from your pout. The answer is simple. The Lover of Your Soul, the One who loves you most. Yep, that's who.

Jesus is the ultimate bridegroom as well as the prototype for what you're looking for in a man. He always responds to your love. He never rejects you. He always accepts you just as you are and keeps His promises. He never lies and He always covers you—protecting you and providing for you. He lives for you, and He died for you. Yes, He loves you! Your relationship with your Creator is the most important love affair you can ever have. There is a God-sized hole in everyone's heart that only He can fill. Without this relationship firmly established, you will look to the wrong sources for completion so you will never find it. And how frustrating is that!

The bottom line is we're not perfect so we fail one another. We can use that as a reminder of how much we need God and His grace! I strongly recommend you turn to Him for guidance in your search for love. Who would know better what you need, what you desire, and what will truly satisfy you than the One who created you? Get movin', girl. You've got a lot of livin' to do.

Dear Michelle,

I can't remember the last time a man spoke to me. I'm attractive, not overweight, well-groomed, and educated, but so far no takers. I have a very demanding job and travel a lot, so one would think I would get a "hello" somewhere. I'm beginning to feel as if I have an invisible sign on me that wards off men. My friends tell me that men stare at me when they pass by, but I don't see them. Why are they not stopping? Is there somewhere specific I need to go to meet men? And don't even mention church—he is not there!

Flying Solo

Dear FS,

It sounds as if all the right things are in place, so why the disconnect? A simple word comes to mind: openness. Be more open. Don't just be interesting, be interested. I can truly relate to your situation and your angst. In his book *How to Find a Date Worth Keeping* (pick it up, I highly recommend it!), Dr. Henry Cloud suggests an exercise that opened my eyes to how closed I'd become when I too was airing your sentiments. You said you travel a lot—good. It's the perfect venue to do this exercise.

Moving through airports opens the door to endless possibilities of meeting people. Become aware of the people around you. Force yourself to make eye contact and smile so men will know it's safe to approach you. Men fear rejection big time like most of us do. Compliment a man on his suit or say something to strike up a conversation that gives him an opportunity to pursue more information about you.

Don't focus on any one type of man. The goal is to get your numbers up, get you back in circulation, and get you comfortable with members of the opposite sex. You don't have to date or fall in love with everyone you meet. Just be open and friendly and let things follow their natural course. Who knows? You might meet Mr. Right, make a friend who introduces you to Mr. Right, or acquire friends who will be and bring blessings to you. Don't close your options! Stay open. One reason someone flies solo is because she didn't invite anyone to take the ride with her.

Happy travels!
Michelle

Keeping It Real

A girl's got to have options. When it comes to life and love, you are more in control than you know. I'm not saying you should pursue a man. That's a big no no. I am saying you should get out there and enjoy life. Say hello to people. Mix and mingle, not in search of anything but for the joy of discovering a life rich with experiences and interesting people. If you do that, you'll be in a position to find yourself surrounded by love—and maybe sooner than you know.

4

The Right Stuff

Quiet as it's kept, the relationships we witness on television and in the movies are fantasies. Let's face it, when was the last time you ran into anyone looking like Ryan Gosling, Bradley Cooper, Brad Pitt, Denzel Washington, or Olivier Martinez? And yet we keep waiting for a gorgeous, flawless man to come into our lives and sweep us off our feet. When I talk with a woman who is still single and hear her laundry list of qualities a man has to have to capture her attention and win her heart, I often think, *This girl is never going to get married until she gets past her list of expectations.*

All right, I know I just saw a flurry of raised eyebrows and necks swiveling. I see you and hear you. "Shouldn't a girl have standards, Michelle?" Yes! You should have standards, but *standards* are different than *expectations*. Good character is a standard; being drop-dead gorgeous is an expectation. Being an AMW (Any Man Working) is a standard; being wealthy is an expectation. Does that clarify things a bit for you?

Far too much time, attention, energy, and dreams are wasted on looking for something that exists in very limited quantities and is often fleeting. Talk about looking for love in all the wrong places! That gorgeous man won't be gorgeous for long if his personality is ugly. And passing time changes what everyone looks like. And how much of what we see is surface only anyway?

Let's forget about what the man looks like for now. Forget about the ugly socks he's wearing or the fact that he's a real fashion victim. Forget that his awful shirt distracts us away from the fact that he might be a really good man. Let's face it, it's easier to change an outfit than it is to rearrange someone's character. In fact, this brings me to an important question. Tell me, my sister, what do you want your *relationship* to look like? Not the man—the relationship. Here's some important advice I'm sure you've heard before, but it's worth repeating: Don't judge a book by its cover. I've seen many beautiful covers with horrible contents, haven't you? So let's get real about what we really want and focus on attracting that into our lives. Beyond that, being able to recognize what we really want and appreciating it when we see it is crucial. When talking to the wives of almost every couple I've admired, the wife has said, "Honey, he didn't look like that when I first met him." Here's one of my guiding relationship principles to keep in mind: A woman is the period on the sentence of a man's life. We complete them, we polish them, we help them. Therefore, let's concentrate on what a man truly needs to be bringing to the party of your life.

A woman is the period on the sentence of a man's life. Women complete men.

The Bible says "charm is deceptive, and beauty is fleeting" (Proverbs 31:30). And that's not just in the case of women but men as well. Not a truer proverb could be spoken. Keeping this in mind, moving past a fine visage and a silver tongue, what else do you want in a man? What is truly essential to your well-being for the rest of your life? What qualities would give you more joy, more peace, and more security in your romantic relationships? Perhaps your answers will help you be open to considering a very different type of man than the ones you've been attracted to in the past.

For a long time I was a self-professed "cougar." I dated young and beautiful men. But now, to my absolute astonishment, I've been completely overwhelmed by an older man! How did he steal my heart before I could size him up against my unrealistic list? By being everything I was really looking for. He charged into my life being kind, generous, warm, attentive, sensitive to my needs, interested in my whims while being wise, consistent, and, well, need I go on?

Chile, I threw my "cougar" list right on out the window! I know a good thing when I see one, especially after experiencing far too many disappointments because of what I'd chosen before. Notice I said "I'd chosen." It's true. Until now, I never stopped to consider what was really important to me and what I wanted my love relationship to look like. I'd been too focused on having "arm candy"—emotionally expensive "ornaments" rather than a good man of solid integrity.

After cycles of dating the same type of man in different sizes, shapes, and colors, I finally realized the only thing that was changing was the name I called them by. The basic characteristics remained the same: slick, commitment phobe, charming but shallow, tons of good intentions with little follow-through, selfish, spoiled, and so on. I had to get sick and tired of being sick and tired to finally figure out that a fine exterior was not enough. I needed *and wanted* substance. I wanted a man who found me more beautiful than himself. I'm not bashing good-looking people. I'm just saying if that is your only criteria or your primary one, you aren't looking for all God has in mind for you.

We're talking about looking for the right qualities. What are they? The stuff that allows you to be your authentic self in your relationship. The stuff that allows you to have what I call an "organic experience" with your man. Let me explain. Being with him is so comfortable you feel at home. You can do anything, say anything, and know you'll still be liked and loved. The right stuff includes him being a man you can trust with your heart because he is trustworthy, he keeps his promises, and he makes you a priority in his life. He brings out your best qualities because he is such a good man. He is kind, generous, and sensitive to your needs and the needs of others.

I'm sure you can add a few things to my list, but the bottom line is how do you want to feel for the rest of your life? Content and happy or filled with angst and disappointment? What have you been experiencing in the past in your relationships? Perhaps it is time to make some different choices to get different results.

I say get clear about your list so you will recognize the best man for you when you see him coming. Don't get distracted by the wrong shoes or socks. Look deeper and see the man beneath the outer layer. There's a reason Beauty fell in love with the Beast. That's not to say your man will look like a beast. Perhaps he'll be easy on the eyes or nothing to shout about on the outside. Ah, but love transforms a man who is just "okay" into the finest thing walking if he makes you feel like a queen. The Bible clearly states Jesus was not handsome. But I bet if you interviewed the women who followed Him, they would say He was beautiful. Why? Because He touched them in a profound way beneath the surface. When He looked into their eyes, He looked into their souls. When He spoke, His words went directly to their hearts.

In your search for Mr. Right, be open to the possibility of getting what you want but perhaps in a different package than you've imagined. Most happily married couples will tell you that the person they married was not their usual "type." We all have a type in mind, but that doesn't mean it's the best type for us. I hear many sisters say they won't consider anyone outside of their race, but love comes in all colors. And sometimes you have to color outside the lines to create a beautiful picture. If you really want to experience love, keep your options open and walk with open hands and an open heart.

On the spiritual side, I've heard women essentially say, "My man has to be the priest of my home." I'm still trying to find this mandate in Scripture. Jesus is the high priest of your home. Your husband is ordered by God to imitate Christ by loving you the same way Christ loved the church and gave Himself for it. This is talking about covering you, loving you, taking care of you, fighting for you. Again, the standard here is to find a *godly* man, not necessarily a super Christian or a bishop.

There are a lot of "men of God" who haven't made good husbands. I'm just keeping it real here. Don't get hyper spiritual and miss out on a good thing. Find a man who loves God and is submitted to Him. If the man won't break God's heart, he won't break yours. The evidence of a Spirit-filled man is that he consistently displays the fruit of the Spirit. You know the list from Galatians 5:22-23—love, joy, peace, forbearance [patience], kindness, goodness, faithfulness, gentleness, self-control. Now that's a mouthful.

If you find a man doing all of that, don't let him get away! All I'm really saying is look for a man who has integrity, sound character, and who is sincerely here for you. Those basics can go a long way. And who knows, perhaps with your consistent influence in his life he might flourish into a super Christian or you may find you love him just the way he exercises his faith quietly through consistent goodness to God and to you. That doesn't sound bad at all.

Dear Michelle,

Where have all the good men gone? It seems I only meet extremes—either fine as wine or homely but nice. I can't fall in love with someone I'm not physically attracted to, but the ones I'm attracted to are not serious about being in a committed relationship. I look around my church and don't see anyone I would give the time of day to.

I meet a lot of interesting men who aren't interested in God, which is a deal breaker for me. This makes my options extremely limited. I have to admit I do like a little trash with my class, but it seems the trash always gets me in trouble! All I want to do is settle down into a safe relationship and have a family. I don't think that's too much to ask. So why is it so hard to find someone who wants the same thing?

Perplexed in the City

Dear Perplexed,

You suffer from a common disease many women share. What your eye is drawn to doesn't match your heart's desire. Even your letter is conflicted. What has ever been safe about trash? How can you know you're not overlooking a good brother at church if you don't even give him the time of day? You've crossed off a bunch of people based on their surface alone.

The deepest loves there ever were evolved over time. No lightning bolts struck. There was no immediate chemistry, but as friendship grew sweet love deepened. How about just befriending a few decent brothers to see what happens? If you've been letting your heart down by following your eyes, you're doing yourself a major disservice. Dr. Henry Cloud, author of *How to Find a Date Worth Keeping*, suggests that if you go out with someone and you don't hit it off, you should go out again unless your displeasure was extreme or something terrible about the person's character came to light. Since people are usually a little uncomfortable on their first time out together, doing it again gives grace for nerves and humanity. Just remember this goes both ways. You won't always be at your best either on a first date. You deserve a second chance too. The bottom line is true love grows. It takes time. And because it grows deep, it looks past the silly things that aren't important in the long run. If God, who sees every imperfection in us, loves us anyway, who are we to insist on perfection in another human?

So where are all the good men, my sister? They are out there. They just might not be wrapped in the package you expect. Step closer, look deeper, and allow for flaws. After all, that's what makes every work of art interesting.

Epitha (be open),
Michelle

Keeping It Real

Time has a way of maturing us and bringing what is truly important to light. At the end of the day, it's not what the man looks like but how he treats you. There is no way you can resist the power of love and kindness if you have a heart beating in your chest. Superficiality only goes so far before the ugly truth is revealed that pretty is as pretty does. We love because God first loved us. As a woman, when a man truly loves you it stirs your desire for him and gives you security. It is God's will for a man to treat a woman (and a woman to treat a man) in a way that makes His love for us visible. So let's start by being clear on what we want and then aligning our focus so we'll be drawn to what lines up with standards that are sound, right, and realistic. You know...God's standards.

5

Mind over Palpitations

Emotional baggage. Everyone has some. You just have to decide what size bags you're willing to carry around—steamer trunks or hand luggage. At some point in time you need to unpack the contents, organize it, and discard what stands in the way of getting the love you want and deserve. Full bags leave you with no room to receive anything new. Hanging on to old hurts and disappointments can set you up for new, fresh ones. It's sooooo important not to superimpose your past over your present. To do so guarantees you will destroy your future. Generally speaking, many women find themselves caught in repeat cycles of disappointment that lead them to draw certain conclusions about life, love, and men. But attitudes and beliefs shouldn't be shaped on just the basis of a person's experiences because that is very subjective and leaves no room for faith.

What you believe affects your attitude and responses to others. Your responses will influence their reactions and set the course of your interactions. For example, if you believe all men are unfaithful, your attitude will repel every man you meet. You will constantly be on guard, and the wall around your heart will be impenetrable...if a man even wants to tackle it. The man will feel your resistance and back off. Then you might walk away saying to yourself, "I knew he was just trying to play me." And the guy has gone off shaking his head, wondering what your problem is and why you were so unfriendly. And the entire time you're none the wiser that you were the one who chased him away.

This may happen more times than you expect. You may be unaware of the extent of your body language, responses, and expressions because you're bogged down by baggage you haven't unpacked. Fear can be real but not warranted. Your emotions can trick you if your main point of reference is past bad experiences. This is when you need to take the time to open up those bags, unpack them, look over the contents and the context, and own your stuff, girl. Even if all those men were bad news, you chose them—and that was *your* part in your love drama. But let's go deeper. What have you learned from your past experiences? Being careful with your heart and being paranoid are two different things. When you guard your heart, you allow enough time to pass for the man to earn your trust. Patience is a tool that uncovers deceit. Paranoia, on the other hand, imagines what doesn't exist until it manifests. It shuts up shop before someone can enter long enough for you to know him. Oh, the missed opportunities! Paranoia is a robber. It is the best friend of fear, and as such isn't satisfied until you're depressed, alone, and bitter.

I recall watching a movie about two people who meet and fall in love. The woman had weathered many disappointments in love and settled into the concept of being alone for the rest of her life when this man came along. At one point in the movie, he was supposed to meet her at a certain time and place. Unfortunately, he had a mild heart attack and was carried to the hospital. He had no way of letting her know. She waited at the meeting place until she could wait no more. She left brokenhearted, concluding her former fears were right. In the days that followed, the poor guy is trying diligently to reach her. She is refusing his calls and running from her own pain. He finally goes to her place of employment and corners her with his explanation. She says something so profound. She tells him that she'd grown so used to being disappointed that she was angry at him for disturbing her. She thought it was safer to live with what she knew than venture beyond it to find the love she wanted.

So many of us live in that space. We're like the woman at the well (John 4). We've suffered so much loss and heartache that it's hard to recognize a good thing when it's finally before us. We're blinded by our disappointment. If this is you, open your eyes, girl. Every day is new and full of opportunities to realize your deepest longings—*if you remain open* to them.

Be honest with yourself about your heart condition, your attitudes, and your beliefs. Do the work necessary to renew your mind and heart in Christ. Just because something negative happened in a previous relationship doesn't mean it has to happen again. Though the signs might be familiar, tell yourself, "This is not the same as last time. This is a different person, I've grown, and God is with me." That old situation hurt you, but this situation might work out completely different. Give the current man a chance to rise and fall on his own merits instead of on the basis of what the last man did.

Don't chase away the very thing you want.

Though you grow from your mistakes, you also want to make sure you're not held in bondage to them. Learn the lessons, adjust your position as needed, and move on with an open mind and heart. Perhaps you'll no longer fall in love after one conversation. That's okay. You're wiser for your past mistakes. You now allow more time to pass before investing your heart. You've learned how to communicate your needs and recognize when a situation isn't the best. You're empowered to give grace for a man's humanity without being a victim of it.

You realize people are flawed, including yourself, so you give as much mercy and grace as you would like to receive. Now when I say this, I'm not talking about putting up with things that are unacceptable or hurtful, such as selfishness, lack of consideration, dishonesty, abuse. You know what I mean. Don't use fear as an excuse not to work through issues that can be fixed with communication. All I'm saying at the end of the day is don't chase away the very thing you want. Do what you need to make your baggage manageable.

Your load should be getting lighter every day as you grow, and that should be showing in your demeanor. Your countenance will be an invitation to connect with you when you encounter someone, whether the relationship turns out to be platonic or romantic. People will want to be part of your world, but that will only happen when you've freed yourself to celebrate life and love without inhibitions. Then your life will be a healthy, fabulous party everybody will want to attend.

Dear Michelle,

Sometimes I wonder if I have an invisible sign on my back that says "Hurt me please!" Every relationship starts off nicely enough, but the ending is always the same. I get dumped, and it's always my fault. I've been told I am too jealous and controlling, but I don't agree. The men in my life all seem to be players who can't be trusted. I let them know I'm nobody's fool so don't even try me.

They got angry because I caught them in their deceit. Believe me, catching them doesn't make me feel any better. I'm extremely sensitive and can sense when something isn't right. And, hey, as the DJ said, I have the gift and I've got to use it! I just wish my gift could find me a man who doesn't end up playing the same old games. I would hate to think that all men are the same, but that's the way it's looking to me.

Still Keeping Hope Alive

Dear Still Hoping,

If it's true that faith is the substance of things hoped for and the evidence of things not seen, then hope doesn't waste its time looking for things that it doesn't want. You've probably heard the song that says if you're looking for trouble, you've come to the right place. If you look for trouble, you're sure to find it.

Exactly what are you hoping for? To be proven right that men can't be trusted? Or to take a leap of faith that perhaps the man before you is honest and faithful? What would your attitude be toward that man if the latter were true? You would be a lot more positive and loveable, wouldn't you? And that behavior would bring out the best in your man. Perhaps...just perhaps...you wouldn't push him away or over the edge with accusations that might encourage him to fulfill your prophecy.

I'm not saying it's a woman's fault when a man becomes unfaithful. Some men have unfaithful spirits. But we must check to make sure we're not providing catalysts or excuses for that behavior. Men for the most part don't want to complicate their lives. They basically concentrate on one thing at a time. Remember that. A man will only eat snacks if he is hungry—not when he is full, if you get my drift. So make sure you are associated with wonderful feelings in his mind and heart, not angst or distrust.

A wise woman knows she doesn't have to let others know she isn't a fool. That should be evident in the choices you make and how you live. File your knowledge away and give the relationship time to grow. Trust me, sometimes things are not what they seem. If you are truly keeping hope alive, stay focused on what you're hoping for instead of what you fear. You attract what you focus on as well as what you value.

I encourage you to change your point of view!

Hoping you give love a chance,
Michelle

Keeping It Real

Anyone who has gotten something she aspired to took a risk. Love is more than a decision. It is a risk—a blind leap of faith or the ultimate bungee jump, if you will. That brings to mind a beautiful picture! Take the leap and entrust the cords of your heart to God. He is able to keep you from hurting yourself. Stop jumping to your own conclusions. Seek God for the inside info on the person you're considering and then listen to what God reveals. Peace is the confirmation of God's plan for your life. When you don't have peace, do nothing. Don't move forward or release your heart to someone until you have God's peace. When you have His peace about the relationship, don't anticipate problems. Believe in the power of love and the power of God to keep your heart and your relationship healthy and satisfying. What it takes to get your man is what it takes to keep him—and it boils down to faith.

6

The Man/Woman Thing

All right, people, listen up. I've got a news bulletin. Contrary to popular belief, we are not so unisex after all. Yes, my friends, men and women *are* different. And that is a good thing if you understand what that means in the realm of relationships. Man and woman were not designed to be the same. If both partners were alike that would make one unnecessary. John Gray points out how different we are. In his popular book, he said men were from Mars and women were from Venus. All joking aside, we are different, and our differences make life interesting and more effective when we embrace them.

Generally speaking, men are moved by what they see and women are moved by what they hear. Men use fewer words than women. They walk differently. They talk differently. They emphasize different activities and priorities. They measure their success and sexuality by their ability to lead, to be productive, to achieve, and to provide for themselves and others. Women tend to define their sexuality by relationships. They also can bear children, which significantly impacts their lives. They respond to many issues differently than men do. Women are more transparent regarding their emotions, and they're more attuned to body language. Men tend to separate emotions from situations a bit more. That said, both men and women make decisions based on logic and emotion in varying degrees.

Definitely men and women view sex and relationships very differently. I often suggest that when women are trying to figure out men, we should think of how we would respond and then do the opposite. Of course, this is very tongue-in-cheek, but the reality isn't far from that truth. Men and women were created and specifically wired by God to focus on different things that require different skill sets.

When we look at male/female differences, we aren't trying to measure or determine equality. We already are equal, although our strengths and weaknesses are different and complementary. Those strengths and weaknesses are what make us need one another. This is why wise King Solomon wrote, "Two are better than one, because they have a good return for their labor" (Ecclesiastes 4:9). Winning teamwork is when team members in the game function in their strengths. The players don't try to take over someone else's position. They stay in their lanes, yielding to and taking advantage of the other members' strengths and positions. No one is focused on who gets credit; winning is the goal. When the game is won, they celebrate together.

Let's get a basic understanding of what the male/female roles are when it comes to humans. Now don't get excited and jump the gun. Bear with me on this because I'm taking you somewhere. God made man first. Then God made Eve. He gave them both specific instructions: to subdue evil, take dominion over every living thing, be fruitful and multiply (Genesis 1:28). To effectively carry out every part of this God-given assignment, Adam and Eve would need and depend on each other.

Man was given a role that, in my opinion, is the most difficult. He was given *authority*. He was held responsible for taking care of God's creation, which included woman. Small wonder the Bible states that if a husband doesn't treat his wife properly, his prayers may be hindered (1 Peter 3:7). That is deep. God is very protective of woman.

I've never understood the great dilemma over women being told to submit to their own husbands, which we will dig into later. I've always focused on the fact that woman was given an even greater power than authority. That's right—she was given the *power of influence*. Influence is more powerful than authority! God has all power, might, and authority, yet He was secure enough in Himself to give mankind full reign over his own responses to God's commands. God allows us to be influenced by our hearts and minds as opposed to making us His robots or slaves. Why do I say *influence* is more powerful than authority? Our hearts and will influence us to sin even in the face of God's ultimate authority. We become slaves to whom or what we worship and serve. That is powerful. Ultimately, how we use our influence can help us live free in Christ or live as slaves.

A woman can make or break a man with her influence. Most women are completely unaware of their own power, yet men are very much aware of it. We women spend more time trying to figure out how someone is trying to devalue us, hold us down, or rob us of our equality than we do celebrating the power we've been given naturally and spiritually and using it correctly.

What is there to celebrate about our differences? Plenty!

What is there to celebrate about our differences? Plenty! For clarity's sake, when the Bible says that women are the "weaker sex," I believe God is not talking about intellect or emotions. No, He's referring to physical strength. Let's face it. We are built differently by divine design for different tasks. In light of how we're built and the roles we've been given, it is the man's assignment to take care of the woman. That's fine by me. I don't want to lift or bear a heavy burden if I don't have to. Whoever gets the assignment from God gets the grace to carry it out. So let's let them. I like it when men open doors for women, pull out chairs for them, and treat them like queens. That leaves us in better shape and with greater desire to treat them like kings.

The truth of the matter is women and men complete one another. While opposites attract, it is still our commonalities that keep us together. So let's take a look at some specific differences and then look at what we have in common.

First, men have been wired to protect and provide for the women in their lives. Women are wired to nurture and serve. Woman was created for man (1 Corinthians 11:9). This is not a terrible thing. God simply recognized the need of man for a good woman. This is why it says that a man who finds a wife finds a good thing and obtains favor from the Lord (Proverbs 18:22). The opposite is also true. If a husband has a bad wife, she can wreck his world and influence him to lose his integrity and the favor that comes with it.

This is really a statement that a good woman adds to a man's life. How? By encouraging him mentally, spiritually, and physically to deal with his world in the right posture and character. A good woman influences her man to be the best he can be. She helps him live up to his God-given potential. You can be like Esther, who influenced her man to save a nation, or you can be like Delilah, who influenced her man to destroy his destiny.

I once saw a sign in a health club that said, "You are only as strong as your weakest muscle." Well, a man is stronger when he has a good woman behind him. Just as the church or believers in Christ are to glorify God and reflect what His presence, goodness, and power look like, a wife is the glory of her husband. She is the evidence of his achievements and his walk with Christ. Her countenance and demeanor let people know if her man is taking care of business the way he should. She is a testament to his faith and character. This is why a man who has little depth looks for "arm candy." He thinks she will validate his masculinity. Not! It takes more than that. The husband needs to be walking with the Lord and following His precepts. The man's life needs to reflect God's values and guidance in his speech, behavior, choices, and overall attitude.

In this discussion on male and female, we're not talking about boys. We're talking about men—men who are mature enough to discern the will of God, follow His wisdom and guidance, know the bottom line of situations, and make sound decisions for the welfare of himself, his woman, and eventually his family. He protects his woman on every front. He cherishes and loves her the way Christ loves the church.

Have you noticed the Bible doesn't command a wife to love her husband? She is to *respect* him. Women don't have to be told to love. This is something we do automatically. Only when we've become disappointed or hurt by men do we lose respect for them. Once respect has been ruptured, our desire and passion for our men are diminished, and this can spell the beginning of the end for a romantic relationship.

But back to the man for now. The husband is told to love in a way that reflects how precious his wife is. His love is to be unselfish and sacrificial, putting his wife before himself to honor her and provide for her. He is to work toward helping her feel secure enough to flourish.

When a woman understands her worth and her power in this romantic relationship, she becomes a force to be reckoned with. Her influence affects her husband's character and ability to thrive and be fruitful. Two of the additional gifts she possesses that prove valuable to her man are insight and intuition. These are nurturing gifts that build up a man and help him avoid pitfalls.

In Ghana, a common saying is "The man is the head; the woman is the neck. Wherever the neck turns, the head turns." Let's make sure we are turning in the right direction. Remember, your relationship with your man is not a contest. It is designed to be a reflection of the kingdom of God and the holy trinity, a representation of oneness through love and cooperation. This is how the world was created. We fashion our personal worlds by understanding God and our place in His creation. We increase our participation with God when we choose to willingly die to ourselves and turn ourselves over to Him. In a romantic relationship based on Christ, two people view their differences as an opportunity to form a powerful, cohesive team that lives for Jesus and glorifies God. And that, my friend, is wonderful.

Dear Michelle,

To be perfectly honest, I have yet to find a man who can do what I can. For the most part, I do everything for myself. I even fix my own car, so what do I need a man for? I find the men I date to be weak and clueless about most things.

Where are the real men? And the men I meet are the ones women are supposed to submit to? We're in trouble then!

I am so exhausted. I don't want to take care of everything, but I find I must. Could it be that the lines between the sexes are blurred because nobody is doing what they're supposed to be doing? What's the answer?

Worn-Out Woman

Dear Worn Out,

Small wonder you're worn out. It's hard to be a woman if you're being a man too. We women were not wired for their role, so we can only function effectively for so long in a manly capacity. I believe most female health issues are linked to the stress we subject our bodies to in the name of "sistahs doin' it for themselves." That's just not good.

You're working way too hard. I don't know why you can't find a brotha to help a sistah out, but I suspect you're shutting them down before they get started. In relationships, men seldom jostle with women for position. A man will often abdicate his place first and let you do things yourself if he senses he's not needed. Then he will go off in search of a place or situation that will allow him to be the man he wants to be—whether that's in the form of another woman, work, sports, or whatever. He's going to live his perception of what a man is somewhere. By the time you've said I'll do it myself a couple of times, a brother shrugs his shoulders and gives up.

So often men don't know what to do with women anymore. They are constantly being told through media they're not needed, and many have begun to believe it. If we want to turn this train around, we're going to have to slow down, exercise some patience, and leave room for men to step up to the plate.

Since women have the gift of influence, I suggest you begin by telling yourself that you will not do what a man can do when a man is around. "Woman up" by batting those eyelashes, standing back, and asking, "Will you help me with this?" and when he does, breathe "My hero" and watch him break into a sweat as he searches for something else he can do for you. At the end of the day, a man wants the same thing you want of him—to be a man. Let him...encourage him...support him.

Woman up, girl!
Michelle

Keeping It Real

I've heard it said that, for the most part, mothers raise their daughters and love their sons. I believe this means that girls are better prepared for life in the world than boys are. Mothers tell their daughters they need to learn how to do everything for themselves in case a man never comes along. However, a mother's tendency is to spoil her sons, especially the mothers who treat their sons as surrogate husbands. Some mothers coddle their boys, doing everything for them. These boys go out into the world looking for mothers instead of wives. (Mothers truly need to get back to raising their sons to be independent men, but that's another conversation and book.) Don't lose hope, girl. There are a lot of good men out there who have been taught traditionally so they know how to be good to a woman. Even if they weren't, remember that wonderful gift of influence God gave you? Well, use it or lose it, sister! Men will rise to the occasion to help when given the opportunity. A few simple rules will help you with this:

- Smile sweetly and let the man know what you want or need him to do. Intuition is not his gift, and neither is ESP.
- Be patient. Men tend to not multitask. Don't frustrate him by giving him too many things to do at one time.
- Learn the power of praise. Men respond to the same thing

you do—praise. Honey *always* attracts more bees than vinegar.

- Stop trying to make men be something they aren't. They are not women. They don't relate or respond as we do. In some ways, they are less complex than we are, which should be a huge relief to you. Men are pretty much black and white, while women specialize in subtle shades of gray (this can be maddening for a man).

So as much as possible, ask men to help, be specific about tasks, and don't expect them to be mind readers. Trust me, you'll enjoy having them around!

7

Fact or Fiction?

There are all sorts of myths—or should I say excuses?—for why some women who want to be married aren't. Sit down over any lunch or dinner table with a bunch of single women and hear the dialogue fly. You're bound to overhear snatches of conversation that include "Well, you know men don't like strong women" and "An independent woman is threatening to a man." I hate to disappoint you, but neither of these statements is generally true.

Life can seem like a catch-22 for women. On one hand, we can't wait around for a man to come rescue us so we need to have the ability and knowledge to make a living on our own. But what we gain in professional acumen and achievement can warp our perception of femininity and womanly wiles. From the boardroom to the living room, from the kitchen to the bedroom, the lines can get blurred on a woman's identity, purpose, and priorities.

My humble opinion is that some accomplished women think way too highly of themselves. This brings a lot of confusion to their relationships. I've heard so many women complain that it's hard to be a woman in this day and age. And, like I've said, I believe that is true...if you're trying to be a man. The problem isn't how accomplished some women are. No, the problem is their overall attitude.

I've discovered that men like women who have accomplished great things. Men like to brag to their friends about what their ladies have accomplished. Your accomplishments are trophies for your man. But here is where things can get ugly. If you're so impressed with yourself that there is no room for anyone else to be impressed with you, there is a problem. No man wants to sit and listen to you rehearse all your accomplishments and acquirements. He loves that you're doing all of that, but his primary focus is on your relationship with him and his relationship with you. He cares about how you make him feel and, more importantly, how he makes you feel.

Your man needs to feel needed because he's been wired by God to care about your state of well being. Does that mean you have to "dummy down"? No, it does not. It simply means you need to put your stuff into the correct perspective. Let's face it. At the end of the day, it's not your bankbook, business, and acquisitions that are going to make your heart sing. Work and activities, including all your accomplishments, are what you do, not who you are. If you're talking to your man about business issues and asking for his input, that's fine, of course. But if you're just running down a list of what you've done, you may sound like an opera singer singing "mi, mi, mi." That is downright unattractive as well as undesirable. So flip the script, put yourself in his position, and tell me how you'd feel. How happy would you be if all your man did was talk about himself—what he'd accomplished and what he was doing? You'd feel like an add-on.

I had a friend who had a good man who loved her. But he didn't like listening to her constantly rehearse all that she'd done, bought, and provided for their family. Eventually he abdicated his interest in being a provider and supporting her sense of well-being. He shrugged his shoulders and said, "What does she need me for?" He wouldn't pay for anything because she was always quick to flaunt how much money she had and how self-sufficient she was. Eventually she fell on hard times, and the money didn't flow the way it had. Honey, that man kicked into the provider role big time. He bought them a house, provided regular funds, and started taking care of business in a way that awed her. She told me she was shocked. She didn't know he had that kind of money stashed away or how generous he could be. I told her she'd never given him a chance to show what he had and what he could do because she'd been too busy telling him what *she* had.

The bottom line is that often a man won't fight with his woman to exercise his role in her life. Think of your growing up years and the boys you knew. When they couldn't prove themselves, they often lashed out by punching you or hitting something in a desperate attempt to dominate the relationship. Little did they know that manhood is not about domination; instead, it's about a man handling his business so that his woman respects him and he can provide for both of them. That is what God means when Scripture says that woman is the glory of man. The woman reflects her man's faith, provision, leadership, and presence in her life. She is better off because of his presence (and he is better off because of her presence).

God holds a husband responsible for the care of his wife. The husband is supposed to protect, provide, and cover his wife. As a matter of fact, this thing is so deep that God says a husband who doesn't take care of his wife and family is considered worse than an unbeliever or infidel (1 Timothy 5:8). As I've shared before, God adds that if a husband doesn't treat his wife right, the man's prayers may be hindered (1 Peter 3:7). Some interpret that to mean God won't hear the husband's prayers. It's important to understand that God expects His people to be in the right position of obedience to receive specific blessings in their lives. When we are out of order naturally and spiritually, God will not go against His Word to bless us. The husband is told to love his

> Be upfront about your accomplishments, but allow room for your man to give to you.

wife and give himself for her the same way Christ loves the church and gave His life for her (Ephesians 5:25). As he obeys God and does this, it brings favor into his life and the blessings flow.

Now let's unpack this information a bit and apply it to your situation. If you're going on about your accomplishments, your man may come to view it as belittling or putting down his contributions. Even if you're not doing it purposely, he may feel you don't respect what he does for you and others within his world. I'm not saying you can't be upfront about your accomplishments, just that you need to allow room for your man to give to you. Balance is needed. If you can be a mover and a shaker in the business world and still let your man know he's your hero and vital to your life, you're doing fine. And knowing you love and appreciate what he does, your man will do whatever he can to make you smile. People need to know they're needed and loved, so let him know you feel that way!

Listen up, lady! Make sure your accomplishments don't crowd out your man's accomplishments. What both of you accomplish should be enhancements to your relationship. Love chooses to build up the other person instead of focusing on yourself. And, girl, don't be afraid to say what you appreciate about your man in public (within reason and comfort levels, of course).

It's usually beneficial to keep your business life separate from your personal business. Make time and space for both. Your personal life and relationships empower you to face the world and take care of business with integrity. So make sure your personal life is fulfilling, growth producing, and satisfying. Remember, you work to live not live to work. We live for relationships, so keep your priorities in the right order.

Dear Michelle,

Why are men so insecure? Must I be an invalid so they can take care of me and feel better about themselves? If I sat around waiting for them to step up to the plate, I would be in a very bad space about now. My mother raised me to be strong and self-sufficient. I run my own company, and I can even do the basic maintenance on my technology stuff. After all, what if Mr. Right never shows up? A girl's got to have skills, right?

So where are the men who will celebrate these things instead of taking offense by them? Should I just forget all the stories and dreams about knights on white horses? All the men I meet need to man up.

Frustrated to the Core

Dear Frustrated,

Kudos for all you do, but may I suggest that you don't do some of that stuff if a man is around? Step aside, bat those fabulous eyelashes, and ask a brother if he can help a sister out. I'm not saying play the helpless female; instead, give the guy some room to pitch in and help you. Don't hold it against him if he's not technically inclined; let him offer to get a friend to help him work on it. Give him a chance to find a solution for your dilemma.

Sometimes a man can't "man up" 'cause a woman doesn't "woman up." Sometimes successful, strong women find it hard to admit they like being in control. Our choices reflect our inner attitudes whether we've recognized them or not.

Most men love being a hero, even to women they don't know. So check your attitude, check your posture, check your demeanor, and check your priorities the next time you feel the urge to do something you'd like a man to do for you. And if the men around you don't make a move, take a deep breath and ask sweetly, "Will you help me?" I'm not advocating you be disingenuous. I'm just saying give the men around you opportunities and space to lend a hand. You'll be surprised at their *positive responses, and you may discover it's okay to not be in control all the time.*

Relax, relate, and release.
You can do it, girl!
Michelle

Keeping It Real

God never meant for women to work so hard. He said His yoke was easy and His burden was light. This is an overall statement about life in general, but for the sake of the principle here, let's just say God never wanted any of us to work as hard as we do. Anytime you feel pushed beyond your natural capacity to handle your business, ask yourself if you've taken on an assignment that was never meant to be yours.

Are you going above and beyond the call of duty? Are you trying to prove something to someone? Is the amount of work you're doing worth feeling worn out and frustrated over? The old commercial with the woman swinging the skillet in one hand and a briefcase in the other while telling the world she can bring home the bacon, fry it up in the pan, and still never let her man forget he is a man was a wonderful-but-overwhelming image that I doubt can be maintained without balance and knowing when to let that man step up to the plate. (That commercial seemed way ahead of its time back in its era.) God took into account that He constructed woman in a way that wasn't designed to bear great weight and stress. That doesn't mean women were built to fail if a man isn't present even though we were created physically weaker. When we don't have husbands in our lives, there are other men around willing to help. Brothers, uncles, nephews, friends, and members of our church family can be a wonderful support system for us. But in our efforts to do things ourselves and be independent, we stress our bodies and coping skills unnecessarily. I believe women taking on too much is the reason for the rise in female health problems. God intended for women to have men present who love them and will be with them to tenderly shoulder the load. So I say we should let them!

Dear Michelle,

I've heard you say that we're supposed to let men take care of us. But what if I don't have a man? What if I'm kicking 50, and Mr. Right has yet to surface? Am I really supposed to not function until I have a man to help me? Is my body gonna break down if I take out my own garbage and fix my own car?

I don't consider myself a feminist, and I'm all for being feminine, but where is the balance in all of this? The reality is that men are not stepping up to help. They no longer open doors, pull out chairs, or offer to help carry something unless I ask. They are passive and seemingly disinterested in being the type of men they should be.

Please help me out here. How does a woman survive until she finds a husband? And what about the women who never marry? Hey, I'm just keeping it real. I'm not trying to cause any problems with your theology, but you have some 'xplaining to do!

Worn Out and Disgusted

Well, Worn Out,

I'm shaking my head too, and I realize that if you wrote this letter there are thousands of women asking the same question. This is where balance has to come in. It is unrealistic to put your life on hold until a husband appears. You're right that doing so isn't realistic. And what if a husband doesn't come your way? The reality is everyone isn't going to be married. Your letter is not a slap in the face of faith. It reflects the reality of living in a world where sin has disrupted God's perfect plan and design.

Not to depress you or anything, but to put things into perspective Isaiah 4:1 says, "In that day seven women will take hold *of one man and say, 'We will eat our own food and provide our own clothes; only let us be called by your name. Take away our disgrace.'" Though being single is hardly a state of disgrace, we can fall prey to the pressure of the world that says everyone should have a partner. It's enough to make singles throw up their hands and give up or grow desperate and settle for less than God's best for them.*

Yet within the insufficiencies of life, God is still at work. The Lover of Your Soul, Jesus, is present to fill you spiritually and emotionally. He is well aware of your needs and sends people into your life to fill in the gaps and relieve the strain. Though they may not be your husband, there should be men in your life who will come to your aid in the practical aspects of life, such as when you need someone stronger than you to move something. When it comes to intimacy, you have to continue to ask God for strength to stay pure and not compromise. You don't want to invite more pain into your life for temporary moments of gratification that only cause you to want more.

The bottom line is God meets you where you are and supplies the grace for you to thrive and flourish no matter what your circumstances if you reach out, accept His help, and make the most of it. The choice is totally yours to make. So ask that brother to open the door and treat you like a lady. Let him take the trash out for you while he is at it. Get on with the business of living your life, girl, but include the men God has put in your social circle.

Single or married, God blesses you!
Michelle

Keeping It Real

Life here on earth will never be utopian—that would be called heaven. And while we have that to look forward to, we still need to flourish where we are. A tree doesn't get to pick where it's planted, but it grows anyway. Being without a man is not a valid excuse for refusing to get on with the awesome privilege of living well. Part of living well is making sure your life is balanced. You should have men in your life. I consider the men in my life great treasures. They are fun, supportive, and have taught me a lot about men. They are always willing to help, and they've been major blessings! I hope you have that too.

Do we want a "to have and hold forever amen" relationship? Of course we do! But life doesn't get put on hold or end if you don't get a man. And life doesn't begin when you get a man either. Your life is your life. Live it to the fullest! God knows all of your needs, and He will meet them in amazing and creative ways if you stay open to Him. Jesus came that you might have an abundant life—whether you're single or married (John 10:10 NASB).

8

Friends and Lovers

Okay, all together now: "I'm an adult, so every unmarried man who walks into my life is a potential mate until I decide differently." So what if you "decide differently"? A good generalization to keep in mind is that when a man who is single initially approaches you, he is probably interested in the possibility of a romance with you. That means his first impression of you was positive. He thought, "Hmm…I want to check her out further." Although your initial thoughts may be that he doesn't meet your mate criteria, give him a chance. Don't throw out the baby with the bathwater. You're under no obligation to reciprocate his feelings of romantic interest, but why not see what happens? Even if he doesn't end up being Mr. Right, he may turn out to be a really great friend. And who knows, he might be the one to introduce you to Mr. Right!

"Why do I want to be friends with a man if there's no possibility of romance?" you ask. There are a myriad of reasons, so I'll name just a few of the most important ones. First, if all your friends are just like you that leads to a one-dimensional, boring life. Two, women learn about men best from being around men. Three, interacting with members of the opposite sex keeps you comfortable with them and creates an aura around you that attracts more interest.

Have you ever noticed that the minute one man expresses interest and you respond, all of a sudden a host of men seem to come out of the woodwork and are interested too? There is something that happens to a woman when men are present in her world. Her eyes light up, she smiles more, and there is more pep and sway in her step. Her countenance is different—she appears more alive, vibrant, and interesting. All of this boils down to massive appeal for the men circulating in her presence. She's like a magnet, powerful and attractive. That's what a woman who feels desirable and lovable is. In the church or out, if women go to their girlfriend-centered corners, they lose this valuable contact with men. You need to be out and about so people can see and experience what a wonderful person you are.

As I mentioned, we learn best about men from men. Ask a woman something about a man issue and then ask a man about the same thing. You'll get two very different answers! I've clocked this fact even when I'm shopping. I'll come out of the dressing room or try on a pair of shoes and open myself up to a man's response to what I'm trying on. Usually their response is totally different than what I get from women I ask. I've discovered that most of us women have been dressing for women instead of men! (Let that idea sink in for a bit.)

"But Michelle," I hear you say, "is it possible for men and women to just be friends?" The answer is yes, yes, and yes again. But there are some guidelines for keeping platonic relationships between members of the opposite sex on the right track. This area can be a breeding ground (pardon the pun) for misunderstandings and heaps of hurt feelings. If a man approaches you, give him a chance to impress you. But if, after a while, you decide you're not interested in a deeper relationship, you need to make it clear (be nice!) that you would enjoy being his friend. Yes, he may pretend to go along with that, hoping you'll change your mind, so be careful not to send him mixed signals.

What's good for the gander is also good for the goose. By this I mean don't take advantage of your man friend. Be kind and considerate of his feelings and communicate clearly and often where you are emotionally with him. Don't lead him on or send signals that might make him believe he's gaining romantic ground. Eventually he'll settle into his friend position if you remain consistent and don't leave room for false hope.

If you find yourself in this situation except you're the one being moved to the friendship file, be honest with yourself and keep a clear mind. If he says he just wants to be friends, believe him and act accordingly. What does that mean for you? Don't be more available to him than you would be for the rest of your friends. Some women are under the delusion that by allowing men to sample how it would be to be dating, the men will change their minds and declare their undying love. Being too available to a guy who only wants you for a friend opens you up to more hurt when his romantic attentions are directed to someone else.

Don't try to fill your romance void with your platonic male friend.

Speaking of false hope, you need to guard your heart too. I know far too many ladies praying and hoping and wishing that one of their "friends" would come around to feeling more romantic. A lot of friends become surrogate boyfriends (and vice versa) in the middle of perfectly good platonic relationships. This can cause the relationship to head south in no time flat. The fallout can be devastating. So take a deep breath and resolve to remain realistic in your friendships. That means believe what he says. If he says, "We're just friends," believe him. Trust me, men do know how to say what they want. If you're wondering why he hasn't moved on yet, don't hope or think it's because he's changed his mind about your relationship. He likes you as a friend, nothing more. Don't try to fill your romance void with your platonic male friend.

Once you decide to stop forcing the issue and settle into a transparent and real friendship, men are great friends. Protective...honest...and did I say protective? Yes, and helpful too. They bring out a side of you as a woman you may not reveal very often. And you get to watch how they deal with other women, which will teach you a whole lot more than I can in one book. I call this learning "love smarts." Ya gotta have it if you want to find love and avoid a broken heart.

It's also good to have male friends to help you scope out potential mates. They can size up that new man in your life and give you the low-down in no time flat. And if you have gay friends, they'll let you know if you need to be concerned about your new male friend. If you don't have "gaydar," a gay friend may help you see beneath the surface and help you separate fact from fiction. I recall a gay friend of mine meeting the fiancé of another friend. After we walked away, he said, "So she is going to marry him?" I replied, "Yes, she is!" To which he said, "But why? He's gay!" You could have knocked me over with a feather! I defended my friend and her fiancé. After they were married, his sexual orientation came to light. Indeed, he was gay. It created quite a devastating mess and resulted in the demise of the marriage.

Male friends can help you check yourself out as well. I ask my guy friends all sorts of questions. I get suggestions from them on everything from clothing to relationship issues. They tell it like it is! They cut straight to the chase and will not spare me from the truth. They tell me when a man is lying or when I've made a stupid relationship move. They tell me things from a different viewpoint than my gal pals do. Why not try it yourself?

Now if you've decided a relationship with a guy is on a friendship level, make sure you remain just friends. No "friends with benefits," if you know what I mean. Kissing cousins and friends with benefits are a no no whether you're a Christian or not. Far too many people in the church get sucked into the world's view when it comes to romance and relationships. God's clear standards are often overlooked, ignored, or, perhaps, not known. Sex, which we will deal with in a later chapter, always adds another layer to a relationship and complicates things big time, and that's without bringing in the spiritual component! Stay clear of this quagmire.

Lots of sisters tell me they have a hard time finding good male friends. Perhaps you haven't been open to men who have approached you. Here's a little experiment for you to do. The next time a guy says hello or looks in your direction, be friendly. Smile, say hello, compliment him on something...anything. Start the conversation to let him know you're safe to approach—whether you're interested romantically or not. The key is to make friends and round out your circle of acquaintances.

Do you wonder what you'll talk about? Interview them about themselves. You'll find out what his interests are, what you have in common, perhaps what you can learn from him, what you can add to his life, and what he can add to your life on a friendship level. Besides, you never know when you may need the help of an attorney, a mechanic, or a strong man to help move something.

Remember, every man in your life doesn't have to be a boyfriend. Make conversation and leave the door open for rich friendships. You can even say, "You seem like a lot of fun. We should hang out sometime." Or maybe, "You seem like you'd be a great friend." Keep it light. Let him know you're open to friendship. This is very nonthreatening to men and generally encourages them to be more open to interaction. If he doesn't respond in kind, don't take it personally. He may be in a relationship or have something else going on. Just move on, staying open to new friendships that will make life more exciting and interesting. And guess what? This also makes you a more interesting person who will attract people wherever you go. And that's exactly what you want, girlfriend!

Dear Michelle,

I've been friends with this guy in my life for about three years, and to tell you the truth, I am totally confused. He says that we are just friends, but he doesn't act like a friend. He calls me on a regular basis and freaks out when he can't find me. He takes me out places and cooks for me. He's very touchy feely.

Every now and then he disappears for a while, and that's when I know he has another woman in his life. But when that relationship ends, he's right back here, picking up our friendship where we left off. He has me on an emotional roller coaster. We get along so well, and it feels so right when I am with him that sometimes I wonder if he's not the one. Then I wonder if he'll finally realize this too.

He doesn't discuss the other women with me. Does that mean I'm his plan B? Sometimes I laughingly say we should just give up and be together to test the water, but he's always quick to point out some nebulous reason we shouldn't be together that way.

Can you help me? I don't know what's going on.

Confused in the Big Apple

Dear Confused,

When a man says you're just friends, believe him. Many men do have a plan B file, but you should never allow yourself to be put there. You've got to make yourself less available. If he has any romantic feelings for you, he hasn't been allowed to miss you enough to figure that out. You've spoiled him by allowing yourself to be his "fallback girl."

A boyfriend who isn't a boyfriend and disappears occasionally needs to go to the bottom of your priority list. Don't get this message twisted. Be honest with yourself. You've made this man a surrogate boyfriend to fill in the romance blank in your life. By doing this, you've also put a cap on your heart that hinders or keeps you closed to possibilities for love.

Your relationship feels safe until he goes off and experiments with a new girlfriend. You have to decide that your time, *your heart, and your friendship are worth more than that. It's time to cut the cords and find a new perspective. Don't be available for every call or request. Get a life and see where it takes you. Yes, you will miss him initially. But you need to fill up your dance card with other friends and activities. You'll be much happier and more open to love. If this man decides he's interested in you romantically, let him pursue you.*

Here's to clarity!
Michelle

Keeping It Real

There is a reason God says to "watch over your heart with all diligence" (Proverbs 4:23 NASB). Did you get that? Not just diligence, but *all* diligence! No one is going to care more about your heart condition than God and you. Our humanity ordains that we are selfish. That's what got us all into trouble in the first place. Knowing this going into any relationship, we can leave room for people to find and take pleasure wherever they can. Now don't get too excited, girl. There are limits.

If you decide a relationship with a guy is going to remain platonic, you need to establish boundaries. And it's not that your man friend is being selfish if he's taking advantage of your being alone by taking up all your time and attention. He's simply being human. It is up to you to stay clear and communicate the reality of what the relationship is all about. Tell him that if you're just friends, you'll treat him like you do the rest of your friends. That means no extra benefits or considerations.

If you're the one on the receiving end of "being friends," don't harbor hopes that might never materialize. If you feel yourself heading down that street, back up and remind yourself what the situation is. Don't visit that corner of your world as often until you get a grip on your heart.

And last but not least, do to others as you would like them to do to you. Don't lead that man down a garden trail because it's comfortable and convenient for you. You will reap what you sow, and sending mixed signals can really complicate relationships. Don't send them… and don't receive them.

9

Love Web Style

Love as we once knew it has taken on a whole new persona in the age of technology. Never before has man and woman been able to have so broad a reach out into space and around the world to find love. Wherever I go to speak to singles, during the question-and-answer segment of the program the same question comes up: "What do you think about internet dating?" Now, you know there are all sorts of things set up these days to help people find and connect with one another. They range from singles functions to cruises, from outings to speed dating, and now there are internet matchmaking organizations galore. The internet burgeons with opportunities of every kind. Websites specialize in finding mates from various people groups, including millionaires, religious faiths, nationalities, gay people, straight people—you name it and there's probably a website for it.

Let's face it. We were created for relationships. If you're out of high school and college, I'm sure you've noticed it's harder and harder to meet new people you might be interested in. Getting caught up in the rat race of life isn't conducive to continuing the social lives we experienced when we were younger. For the most part, you go to work, go to church (perhaps), go home, and that's it. During the week you're too exhausted after work and fighting traffic to think about hanging out. If you do, it's usually within the safe confines of a group of coworkers or girlfriends. Being with a group of people can make it hard for any man who might be interested to approach you because he's afraid of being rejected in front of the group or assessed by everyone.

Where is a woman supposed to find someone in this day and age? Obviously you've looked around your church and may or may not have seen a few prospects and didn't find much interest. Work isn't the best place to look, so what's left? Yep, you got it—having someone set you up on a blind date or turning to the internet. Does this mean you aren't trusting God's timing or providence? I think not. If God can use a donkey to give His prophet Balaam direction, He can certainly use other people or tools to help you meet someone (Numbers 22:21-34).

I don't have a problem with using the internet for meeting people. My brother met his wife that way, and she's fantastic. Based on this, I do have a few observations to share if you're going to take this route to find Mr. Right...or should I say *be found* by Mr. Right? Why do I say *be found*? Because I think the same principles apply whether you meet men in person or make contact using social media. The bottom line is that I've heard just as many good stories as horror stories about people who met in person as I have from people who met through the internet. Therefore, I think it's safe to conclude that wisdom must guide you no matter how or where you meet someone.

So let's talk about your position when it comes to using the internet to meet someone. First, I don't have a problem with you posting a profile of yourself. After all, you need to position yourself to be found. When you read the story of Ruth in the Bible, she wasn't found by her man inside a house. She was working in a field. She was out doing something with her life. She wasn't looking for a man; she was *found* by Boaz while she went about her business. After he showed interest, she let him know she was interested in him. That should be what you're doing. So post your profile and stay put. I don't recommend you browse through potential candidates and select men to contact. I recommend you *respond* to those who reach out to you. Remember, the man is supposed to find you and, if interested, pursue you. You always want to be and feel chosen.

Second, guard your heart. Don't fall in love with a photo, or a note, or even a video interview. Pictures can be deceiving. You don't know if the picture is current or even of the actual person. Notes can be collaborations, exaggerations, or outright lies. Anybody can write one. You need to check to see if the man backs it up personally. Remember Cyrano de Bergerac? He started out wooing someone for a friend. Videos can be rehearsed and scripted. All I'm saying is talk is cheap. You need to know what's real about this person *before* you allow your heart to get involved. You need to meet the men in person in a public arena (for safety). Have conversations. Observe them in their element. Meet their friends. (We'll talk more about the ins and outs of dating in the next chapter.)

Technology does not a romance make. This is important to note because we women are moved by what we hear or read, while men are moved by sight (or should I say *site*?). Men will select you based more on your photo, while you will be moved more by their descriptions, cute quips, and remarks. If he's a good communicator or has had someone help him prepare, you might listen to him and think, "Aw, he sounds so sweet!" But on what basis are you assessing him? You don't know if anything is real yet! And, girlfriend, I'm speaking from experience.

Some years ago, a well-meaning friend connected me to a brother she thought was perfect for me. (I know—scary, right?) The man sent me the most beautiful emails. I couldn't wait to meet him! He sounded like the best thing next to sliced bread. Finally the day came when my travels took me to his city. He came over to see me right away. He was cute enough, nice enough, and all that, but we were poles apart in terms of the basics. My heart dropped to the floor. I knew this was not a match made in heaven by any stretch of the imagination. There was no attraction and conversation was difficult—even though we'd been jammin' by email.

One website that provides as much information as possible for users, and thus would do a good job slowing your roll, is eharmony .com. Years ago I met Dr. Neil Warren, the founder, as well as Les and Leslie Parrot, the psychologists who formulated the questionnaires the website uses to establish your profile and match you with someone. These wonderful people had the right idea! How can "two walk together unless they have agreed to do so" (Amos 3:3)? Dr. Warren's philosophy was simple and scripturally based. The more you have in common with someone, the better you will get along. I agree! No wonder this has been touted as one of the most successful sites at putting people together. I attest to knowing countless eharmony couples who have gotten married. The test, if you're strong enough to get through the entire thing, does a lot of the weeding out for you. Of course, nothing is foolproof, and a person does have to tell the truth for the site to truly work.

Now, back in the day when I tried it out while doing research for a television show, the website didn't reveal someone's photo until you reached the last level of exchanging correspondence and answering a series of scripted questions with your match. Nowadays you get to see the photo up front when you're informed you have a match. At this point, remember not to judge a book by its cover.

The internet is a creative way to broaden your world without having to leave home.

Wait for the contents to come. Take your time getting all the information you can on the person you're considering *before* you engage your emotions. Going back to my brother and his wife, they did it right. First, they went online looking to broaden their network of friends, not strictly looking for a partner. With this approach you can't be disappointed if you don't land a husband but end up with a couple of great new and interesting friends. After they emailed back and forth for a while, they began talking by phone because they lived in different cities.

When she eventually moved to the city he lived in to be closer to her parents, my brother was dating someone else. He considered the online match a great friend. About a year after her move, the light came on, and they were married shortly thereafter. All of that to say they were friends first and felt no pressure to like each other romantically just because they met through an online dating service. In the end they both married their best friend, which is as good as it gets. They are still happily married after more than ten years! That's what I'm talking about—the end goal is to marry your best friend, whether you met online or not.

If the internet is a medium that works for you, go for it. Much of my life is spent in front of a computer, so it is not my preferred means of meeting anyone. The internet dating thing requires a lot of time for interacting, answering queries, eliminating undesirables, and taking risks to weed through the candidates so you can be found by Mr. Right. And, of course, you should exercise caution in meeting any potential suitors. I recommend public venues that are open and safe. Let people know who you are meeting and when and where. Keep the meeting short the first time, whether you like him or not. Ask a lot of questions. Be interested for good reason: You are gathering information. Pay attention to body language. Trust your instincts. Stay pleasant. Keep it light. Sit back and see where the whole thing goes.

In an age that makes it difficult to meet new people unless you have a full social calendar, the internet is a creative way to broaden your world without having to leave home. Just know at some point in time you will have to step out of your world and into the unknown with the person you meet. Exercise the same care and wisdom you would if you met someone at church, a public setting, or through a friend. The internet is a virtual experience; life is not.

Dear Michelle,

I met the greatest man on my Facebook page. He is handsome, wealthy, witty, and everything I've been looking for. But I'm a little concerned. We've been talking for *over six months now, and I still haven't met him in person. We live in different cities, and he has a very demanding job. I consider myself an attractive woman, and he constantly tells me how beautiful I am, but he still hasn't been able to find a window of time to visit.*

Well, I finally went to his city—though not to see him—to visit my relatives. He said he was out of the country but went to the effort to fly back to see me for a few hours. He was everything I imagined he would be—a total gentleman. I was a little surprised by the dining choice—it was a chain restaurant. I thought if he had the kind of money I'd been led to believe he had, he would have selected something a little more special or upscale. But no big deal; I'm not materialistic.

What gave me further cause for alarm is over the holidays he vanished for about a week. He resurfaced saying that he'd been ill, was in the hospital, and didn't have his cell phone. I don't know what to think. Don't hospitals have phones? What do you think?

Not Adding Up in My Mind

Dear Not Adding Up,

This isn't adding up on paper either. I think you already know the answer to this scenario, but here goes. Yes, hospitals do have phones so that was a very sorry excuse for not calling you. During the holidays, you say? That's prime time for any man with a significant other or family he can't ignore. Danger! A big red flag is waving on that one. When a man disappears over the holidays, you need to understand you're not his top priority—someone else is.

Now you tell me this man flew from a foreign country for a few hours but couldn't fly across the same country, which *would have been cheaper and faster, to see you? Come on, girl! Either this man is married or pulling your leg...and possibly the legs of many other beautiful girls at the same time. If he was really interested in you, brother man would have made the time to get to you.*

The fact that he disappeared over the holidays and, before that, was only able to see you for a few hours when you were in his city should tell you everything you need to know. Obviously he didn't take you to his house. And it doesn't sound like he took you to a place he usually frequented, if he'd given you the correct impression of his life. Perhaps he took you somewhere so that if he were seen with you by people he knew it wouldn't look like he was on a special date. Or perhaps he isn't as wealthy as he led you to believe.

I think we've done the math enough on this one. This man is seriously wanting in several categories, including honesty. Kick this man to the curb and keep on stepping. Do not engage.

Can you say "block," as in "unfriend"?
Michelle

Keeping It Real

What you see is not always what you get. Keep in mind that people only present what they want you to see, and this can be even easier in the virtual world of technology. Make sure you guard your heart and do your homework. At the end of the day, your heart and perhaps even your life could be at stake. *Be careful* emotionally and physically. Don't set yourself up for disappointment. Stay accountable to friends during the process of interacting with people you meet on the internet...or anywhere else for that matter. Take the necessary steps to learn everything about the person you meet. Wait to make sure all your findings pan out before you engage emotionally. Then proceed to enjoy yourself and see where the friendship takes you.

10

Dating, Mating, and Relating

Okay, ladies, here is where life gets tricky. Dating should not be a scary proposition. It should be an organic experience where the stage is set for love to grow naturally if it's right or for true friendship to blossom 'cause every man you meet is not going to be your husband. Dating is all about your mindset. It will make it a pleasant experience or a nightmare. Repeat after me:

"Dating is not for mating. It is for collecting data."

You got it—*information*. You need information to decide accurately if this person even qualifies to be considered for courtship. You won't know that on the first date...or even the second one. As my mentor P.B. Wilson always says, "Patience is the tool that uncovers deceit." People can only pretend to be someone else for so long before their true colors come out. And when that happens, you need to believe what you see and not make excuses for it. Decide if those revealed qualities are what you truly want to deal with the rest of your life.

So what's the plan for dating? What data or info are you trying to collect? Well, you've got a lot of homework and fieldwork to do, my friend. I compare dating to shopping. Everyone knows it's detrimental to go grocery shopping when you're hungry. You will either buy things you don't really want or need and end up with buyer's remorse or you will walk away empty-handed because you were too overwhelmed by your need to really be clear on what you wanted. Neither of these is a great option. I say shop with purpose, girl! Be clear about what you're looking for, and don't settle for counterfeits.

I don't know about you, but when I'm shopping I am "oh so serious" about making sure I select things that are of excellent quality. They don't always have to be expensive, but they have to be made to last. To hold up under pressure and extreme conditions. And to make it through the wear and tear of everyday wear. Someone once said it's not the exciting things in life that will undo you, it's how you weather the mundane. So when dating, it is necessary to check out the fabric. Fabric meaning the person's character. What is that man made of?

Does he keep his word? Is he consistent? What about his character? Is he a strong person? How does he handle pressure? Does he need anger management training? Is he transparent in his dealings with you and others? Does he have integrity? All this takes *time* to find out and requires careful observation.

Don't just check him out, either. Check out his friends too. His friends reflect who he is when he's not with you. He agrees with these people. He likes what they like. That's why they are friends. Take note: There is no way you can separate who he is from who his friends are. People are who they are across the board. Very seldom are they able to compartmentalize their character.

Also check out his family. Want to know what he's going to look like and be like in 20 years? Look at his father. Watch how his father treats his mother. That's probably how he's going to treat you. His parents' relationship is his reference point for how a marriage should go. If his parents' marriage isn't a good model, remember that a man whose mind has been renewed by Christ might have an entirely transformed mindset that would then manifest different behavior. Ask plenty of questions to find out for sure. You need to take the time to make sure what he's projecting is a real difference that goes all the way to his heart.

For the most part, we turn into our parents somewhere along the aging process. Check out his mother too. How he treats his mother will also give you a clue as to how he will treat you. If he has unresolved "mama drama" or "baby mama drama," it will be superimposed on his relationship with you.

Consistency is huge! A double-minded man is unstable in all his ways (James 1:8). Don't expect good things to come out of a relationship if he always keeps you off balance by causing you to wonder what he will do next or if he will do what he says he will do. Insecurity is not a good look. You wouldn't wear a garment that has snags and holes in it, so don't wear a relationship like that either.

When I'm shopping and find something I like, the fabric may be great but the next thing I check out is the fit. It's not good enough for the garment to be something I like, it's not good enough for it just to look good. It has to look good on me! It's got to fit right. And it has to be conducive to my activities. I don't need a prom dress 'cause I'm not going to a prom anytime soon—no matter how pretty the dress is!

I've met a lot of nice men, but they didn't all fit into my life scenario. I don't believe in being uncomfortable or tortured—or doing that to others—so when I consider being in a relationship, I need to ponder whether it's going to be good for both of us. If my interest is in doing missionary work in Papua New Guinea with natives, a rock star in Los Angeles wouldn't be a good match. He would want nothing to do with living with natives, and I would want nothing to do with tolerating screaming fans. Where would we live in the midst of such vastly different desires and dreams? One of us would feel robbed in this scenario, and that would translate into resenting the other person. And that's simply not the makings of a happy, satisfied, peaceful love life.

Your Dating Preparation

Dating requires some work on your part before you consider adding another person to your life. That's right. You have to know who you are and what you want out of life before you can align yourself with anyone. If you don't take the time to figure this out first, you will eventually be among the couples saying, "We grew apart." I always wondered about that expression until I came to understand this simply means that someone in the relationship grew into who he or she really was and left the other person, who hadn't grown or was perfectly happy maintaining, in the dust.

The other thing that can happen when you don't do the "who am I" work is you get up one morning and say something else a lot of couples say. They look at their partners and say, "You're not making me happy." Well, duh! It was never the spouse's job to make the other person happy. *Add* to the happy, yes; be the basis of it, no. That is too much responsibility to give to any one person. As a matter of fact, let me help you here. God will never allow any person on the face of the earth to completely satisfy and fulfill you. If He did that, that person would become an idol for you. And God doesn't want you to let anyone take His place in your life. He knows that ultimately He is the only one who will never fail you. He watches over you to protect you. He longs for you to trust Him completely. It grieves Him when you place your trust in things or people instead of Him. God is not greedy about your love; He is protective of your love because he knows the issues of the heart affect your life deeply. He created a hole in your heart that only He can fill. Trying to stuff everything and everybody into that place except Him leads to disappointment and heartbreak every time.

Last but certainly not least, is the area of finance. Though some things may be fabulous, they are simply not worth the price it costs to have them. When I'm purchasing an item, I calculate how much usage I can get out of it for my money. Will it last? Will it be worth my investment? The same is true with relationships. A man may be fine as wine, but if he causes major drama and trauma in my life, I don't have enough of a budget to cover what that will cost my heart or life. How about you?

Anyone who doesn't add to who you are, enhance your life, and bring joy and fulfillment on a whole new level than what you had when you were alone isn't worth the price of admission to your life. If the person costs you friends, family, career, financial stability, spiritual ethics, physical security, or emotional well-being, that relationship is too expensive. You don't have enough in your love budget for that.

Unfortunately, most of the ones who cause people the most stress have the least staying power. They are flashes in the pan who wreak havoc with your heart, mind, body, and soul, and then they depart just as dramatically as they entered. Don't fall for the hype. Take the time to assess what is good for you, what doesn't work for you, what is critical to your well-being, and then stick to your guns. If anyone violates those essentials, you know he is not where you should be investing your time, your mind, and your heart.

No man should ever leave you quivering in a heap of insecurity or low self-esteem. If he isn't adding value to your life, he is subtracting from it and who you were created to be and accomplish. You shouldn't have to wonder if he loves you or if it's your fault every time something goes wrong. You shouldn't have to wonder if you are desirable, lovable, intelligent, and beautiful. Your man should be letting you know you are these things. Remember, the enemy of your soul—the devil—would love to paralyze you with self-pity. Satan's agenda is to destroy your appreciation of yourself any way he can. He wants you to forget what God says—that you are fearfully and wonderfully made by Him.

What is the one thing women tend to say when a relationship doesn't work out? Uh huh, you got it. "What's wrong with me?" How about there may not be anything wrong with you and everything wrong with the man? Could it be the only thing wrong was investing your heart and emotions before you were ready or knew all the facts?

The Bible says to "watch over your heart with all diligence, for from it flow the springs of life" (Proverbs 4:23). Yes, your heart condition can be a matter of life and death. You can't afford to be careless with it or allow others to mistreat it. God holds you responsible for your heart, so handle it with care and protect it better than you would your most valuable possession because that's exactly what it is! So handle your heart and love carefully by living with wisdom.

Dear Michelle,

I think my "man chooser" is broken. I have a knack for picking the wrong guys over and over again. It always starts out soooo good! Lots of good chemistry, you know. But as soon as I decide he could be the one, everything goes south. The man changes! I don't know how to explain it. It turns out he isn't the man I fell in love with. Is it me or him? Am I doing something that makes him turn from a prince into a frog—or worse, into a full-out monster?

My friends say I fall in love too fast and set myself up for heartbreak. But isn't risk involved when it comes to love? I can only go by what I see—a handsome, charming man who later turns into an inconsiderate jerk. Do I sound bitter? Perhaps I am. I will await clarity from you before I make another move.

Scared to Try Again

Dear Scared,

Perhaps you should be—scared, that is. Not that I'm calling you a surface person or anything, but only going by what you wrote, let me see if I can list how you've been choosing your men: chemistry, good looks, and charm.

Well, my friend, the Bible tells us that looks will fade and charm is deceitful. As for chemistry, well it can be downright explosive in a bad way if not combined with the right ingredients. Yes, it is true there are risks when it comes to love that one must be willing to take. But may I suggest that you take informed risks? After all, a heart is a dangerous thing to waste.

To succeed when investing in stocks, a person has to do research to know if the stock is a reasonably safe thing to bet on. The same is true with your heart. Thus my guide for finance, fabric, and fit when it comes to dating includes checking the man out. You need to do your homework, girlfriend, before coming to any conclusions and committing your heart. You need to know if this person is worthy of consideration before you throw your heart in the air and hope he'll catch it and handle it with care. You may find after doing your research that he is not qualified to play the role you want him to play in your life.

And get advice from your friends before you give your heart away. They don't wear rose-colored glasses when it comes to your love life. They are protective and objective parties to your indulgences.

If you are moved by surface qualities, you need to file those away until you get enough beneath-the-surface information. Who is this guy when you look beyond the good looks and hormones? Is he honest? Does he have integrity and sound character? What is his past record with romantic relationships, friends, and employment? And what is he looking for in a relationship with you?

May I dare say that none of those men changed in relationship to you? That you perhaps overlooked their character because you were too wowed by what you saw or felt? Neither of these things will help the accuracy of your long-term judgment. Yes, enjoy the view and how you feel, but hold off on investing your heart until you've gathered enough facts.

There are lots of pretty houses with no one home, if you know what I mean. Get over the surface stuff and be willing to dig deep. Life gets complicated, and you will need someone who can and will want to go through it with you. You deserve that.

Been There, Done That,
Michelle

Keeping It Real

The apostle Paul wrote that when he was a child he spoke and acted like a child, but when he became a man he put away childish things

(1 Corinthians 13:11). The bottom line is that we all need to grow up and get past magical thinking. That kind of approach—believing love happens by osmosis and can be sustained in the midst of bad choices—is, well, naïve and childish at best. Sure Snow White and her prince didn't gather information on each other before falling in love and living happily ever after—but their story is a fairy tale! If we checked on the real-life results of a Rapunzel or Cinderella story, we'd probably find they had a very different ending. The truth of the matter is that you can't rely on just chemistry or even spiritual inklings alone to choose a life partner who will help you achieve marital success and satisfaction. Unless you hear from on high so clearly that "you know, that you know, that you know" it's the voice of God saying, "My child, this is the one!" you'd better not move without gathering information. And remember, God will always confirm His word to you with accompanying signs through His Word, your circumstances, or people. Too many women have said, "He changed" after they said "I do." In retrospect, he was always the person he'd revealed but the woman was so happy to finally have someone's attention that she didn't pay attention to the facts and warning signs.

Repeated occurrences in your life usually point to one common denominator—you. This is a sign that at least part of the problem is on your end—either in your choices or your fact checking. If you want different results, you have to approach dating differently. So slow your roll. Put your heart on hold and get enough information *before* you invest your mind, your heart, and your spirit. All three are extremely vulnerable when longing for love, so place them under wraps and protect them until you're as sure as possible that you've done your homework well.

11

Great Expectations

I'm going to take my time and approach this subject from all angles to make sure you don't miss anything. I want to be clear on this because I've sat through way too many conversations with women who were frustrated for no good reason. Okay, I take that back. They did have good reasons, but their suffering was totally unnecessary. Why? Because they'd painted themselves into corners. They had volunteered to be victims of loneliness! Love isn't painful, people. It is our *expectations* that make love a fertile ground for sorrow and disappointment.

We've all had conversations like this one I had with a sister friend who was bemoaning her state of loneliness.

"What about 'so and so'?" I asked.

"Oh, he was nice, but he just wasn't my type."

"Are you married to your type yet? No? Obviously your type ain't right," I countered.

A friend of mine once said, "We pray and pray for God to send us someone, and then when men approach us we bat them away and say, 'No, God! Not that one!'"

After I finished laughing, I realized that was totally true. What makes us swat away perfectly good life partner candidates? Expectations, that's what. Perhaps he didn't look the way we expected him to look. He didn't have the right car, right job, right bank account, right voice, right approach. His shoes were all wrong. I could go on, but I'm going to stop because imagination is a terrible thing to waste. I think it's best for us to separate our realistic expectations from our personal preferences so we can open ourselves to a world of possibilities when it comes to men instead of eliminating candidates based on nonessentials. Many types of men can make us happy if we give them a chance.

Remember, God said Adam needed help. The man needed a woman who would finish him. Who would polish up his rough edges. Who would put the "James" in "Bond, James Bond," if you know what I mean. Someone who would help him put the "s" in "suave." It's true that many men don't clean up well on their own. Every happily married woman I've ever spoken to about how fabulous her husband is has the same comeback: "Girl, he wasn't like that when I got him!" So there you have it. Small wonder the phrase "behind every great man is a great woman" has become a standard.

Bear this in mind when you're meeting men. There are good reasons to believe that when you meet your potential mate, he might be a diamond in the rough. So don't make hasty judgments or decisions during your first meeting. He might be like a fine wine you need to acquire a taste for. And when you do, there may be no turning back!

Should there be some deal makers and deal breakers on your consideration list? Of course! Don't get my message twisted by thinking I don't advocate having standards. There are some things you need and should expect. There are some things you will not accept and some things that should make you push the pause button until you get clarity. But let's not throw out the bathwater before we really check to see if there's a healthy baby in it! If God has the good sense to look at the heart and not be moved by exteriors, we need to take a clue from that.

Realistic expectations don't include requiring the guy looks like Rob Pattinson, Mario Lopez, Brad Pitt, or Denzel Washington. Or that he has a bank account like Bill Gates does. Those are *personal preferences*. Remember, there are many pretty houses with no one home, no working lights upstairs, or no sane person in residence. What is common is always more available than the rare and valuable.

First, you should expect your potential partner to have a close, personal relationship with Jesus Christ. Next you should expect your dating candidate to have good and solid character. Uh huh. You want a man who means what he says and acts accordingly. God commands your future husband to love you the way Christ loved the church and gave Himself for it. So looking ahead, you can rightfully expect a love like that—a love that is not selfish or self-seeking, a love that is giving and generous. You want a man who will give himself for you, be sensitive to your needs, and have a deep and genuine caring mingled with passionate attraction for you—and *only* you. Now that's some stuff to expect! You should expect a man to be kind and not abusive. You should expect him to have a job.

Do you get what I'm saying? You want a man with good basics that will last a lifetime. Looks change, finances change, even job status changes, but how a person generally handles himself is an indication of how he will finish. Does the man have a vision for his life that he is actively working toward even if he is currently financially strapped? And is he strapped for cash because of uncompromising focus on pursuing his vision or because of laziness? Those are key questions.

Should you expect or look for a millionaire? No. Perhaps he needs you in his life to help him make a million dollars and become a successful businessman.

Should you be looking for someone to rescue you? No. That is not a husband's job description ala God. As a matter of fact, God's job description for a husband says he will love you and care for you the way he would care for himself. Your job description is to respect your husband, submit to him, and help him! (We'll get into submission later.)

Are you only considering men who don't need help? Why? You were created to be a helper for the man (Genesis 2:18). H-e-l-l-o-o-o! That means he can use *your* help! Do I see your neck moving and your eyes rolling? Lest you go to the extreme, I am *not* saying you should go out and find a homeless man who has no vision, no drive, no plan for achieving his God-given potential. I am saying you should desire a man with a solid spiritual foundation, good character, and a sense of destiny. However, you should stop looking for perfection. Perfection doesn't exist in him or in you.

In today's world the options aren't what they used to be. You may need to be a bit more flexible in your expectations, knowing that sometimes God's best for you might come in an unfinished form. Why would God do that? To refine both of you, of course. Sometimes God's best for you might be something you aren't currently looking for at all. Perhaps he's of a different race, an age you hadn't considered, working in a field you hadn't allowed, or is completely different than who you usually go for. And yet if you take the time to get to know this man, he can add to your life in ways you never expected.

Expectations can hinder you from seeing the countless opportunities available. They can lead to the worst form of "One-Tree-I-Tis." You don't want to get fixated on one intangible that won't matter months or even years from now. How does this man make you feel? How does he live his life? Those are aspects you need to be clear on. Do you feel loved and secure when you're around him? Does he encourage you to become a better woman? Is he inspired to become a better man because of his interactions with you? Is this a man you can complement? Can you envision the two of you as a couple doing great things for and through Christ because of the strengths you bring to one another?

These are things that take a while to discover. Finding the right person is a numbers game to a certain point. You have to circulate. You have to gather information that might not be readily obvious. It takes time to find a diamond, and sometimes you have to dig deep.

Dear Michelle,

I met this guy, and he is as cute as he can be. He's witty, fun, sweet, attentive, honest, and truly into me. All qualities I love! But I'm conflicted. You see, I am a vice president of a major company, and he is a plumber. This isn't the kind of career I had in mind for my future husband. His occupation is also not what any of my friends can see my future husband doing. They keep telling me that I am settling.

I've always pictured myself with someone who basically does what I do. This man in my life makes good money and is a great conversationalist, but I get nervous when we go out and people ask him what he does. I can feel the air change in the room after he answers. He is quite all right with his occupation, but I am struggling.

Between my expectations and those of the people in my circle, I feel like I can't introduce him to anyone without getting some kind of negative reaction. And yet I truly enjoy his company. He makes me feel so loved. He is so attentive. He's all the stuff I like, but why didn't he show up in a suit and carrying a briefcase?

So the questions remain. Am I settling? Should I keep holding out for a white knight with a briefcase?

Sincerely,
Emotionally Confused

Dear Confused,

Yes, you are confused. Let me tell you a little story. I know a lady who was a top executive of a major company. She married her gardener! Yes, her gardener. She obviously saw more than the shrubs he was planting at her place, and when she added her finishing touches to his life, he eventually owned a successful landscaping business. What if she'd worried what her friends thought of her man? She would have missed out on a blissful life complete with beautiful children.

At the end of the day, all those people who have opinions about what your life and your man should look like will go home to their own lives that may or may not be as fabulous as yours. This might be a good time to point out that some of them might be jealous of your happiness even if your guy is "just a plumber" in their eyes. You can't live to fulfill other people's expectations or agendas. If you try, you won't attain your God-given goals, expectations, and joy.

I think this would be a good time to make a list of the things that really matter to you when it comes to your relationship with the person who may become the man of your dreams. What do you really want from the relationship? What lasting qualities do you want to see in the man you will call husband? When you're done, line up your "plumber man" to that list and see how he measures up. If he does, I say go for what fulfills you and makes you happy. Next to God, there is nothing more empowering than having a man who makes you smile, feel more beautiful, and loved. Why allow anyone to rob you of that?

Just think about it.
Michelle

Keeping It Real

A fairy tale is what we believe when we're growing up. We're taught to expect a knight in shining armor to appear on a white horse to rescue us. After the rescue, we're supposed to live happily ever after. But that isn't where we really live. The knight in your life might look very different from what you imagined. That is the danger of expectations. You can waste a lot of time looking for something that doesn't exist. There really is no such thing as your "type." Many women spend their lives in pursuit of an imaginary knight.

The reality is you need to be very clear on what you need to go the distance in a long-term relationship. What do you need from another person for the relationship to function at its best? Stop and take stock of what you want your love relationship to look like. Notice I didn't say what you want *your man* to look like. Chemistry and looks will pass, but your marriage established before God will continue on. What others think of your choice of husband won't make a huge difference in the long run if you choose carefully. And make sure you're not holding out for a fantasy while missing a reality that could be a major blessing!

12

In Search of Mr. Right

We spend our whole lives looking for "him," but how do we know when we have finally met our Mr. Right? How do we separate the princes from the frogs? How do we know we've finally met the man who is the real thing? I go back to my favorite book (that would be the Bible) and the various ways people got together, and I see a blueprint emerge with a few tips that will help a sistah out.

I always thought it was odd that God had Adam name the animals before He gave him a mate. Was God having Adam do this so he'd notice that all the animals were in pairs as a subtle hint that he also needed a "plus one"? Was he allowing Adam to see all the choices that weren't right so he'd recognize the right one when she appeared?

Sad to say, many of us aren't ready for men who are really marriage material until we've had our hearts broken several times by "playas." It takes awhile to figure out what won't work for us before we can recognize what will work. Don't ask me why; that's just the way it is. And in the Bible, all we're told is no suitable mate was found for Adam within the animal kingdom. And yet today a lot of women settle for "dogs" and "frogs" instead of waiting for the good men. Could it be these women don't know what they're supposed to be looking for?

Desperation is another factor that stops many a woman from doing her relationship homework well. As the saying goes, "One who is full loathes honey from the comb, but to the hungry even what is bitter tastes sweet" (Proverbs 27:7). It is important to be in a state of contentment about yourself and your status before entering the dating arena or you will end up with someone you don't really want or need. It's like when you go grocery shopping on an empty stomach. Everything looks good, including the foods that just aren't good for you. You neither needed nor really wanted them, yet in that moment of hunger you didn't use the best judgment and chose to take unhealthy food home. The same can apply to dating. As delectable as some men may be, some are bad for your health while others are good for you. How can you know the difference? There are telltale signs that signal if this man should be on your radar and worthy to be considered not just as your beau but as your Boaz. There are several qualifiers you should have on your basic list. After that, be open to the things that aren't carved in stone, such as looks, job description, and attire choices. Those items generally have little bearing on his character.

So what are the qualifiers? First, does he love God? I'm not talking does he know *about* Him, but does the man *know and love* God? Is he submitted to Him? If he is, this is a man who won't break your heart because he doesn't want to break God's heart. He will be sound in character because he knows he'll be answering to God not only for his actions but what he also did to and for you. A man who walks in healthy fear of God will be careful with your heart. A man who consistently walks with God, knows His Word, and has taken it to heart will understand his role in your life as a friend and, if it progresses to that, as your husband.

Second, the man needs to have a healthy love and respect for himself. The man who loves himself will love you and take care of you the way he would himself. Hey, that's scriptural too! He will be sensitive to your needs because he isn't thinking about what he lacks. He has a healthy outlook on life and what he has to offer to you and the rest of the world. He is a whole man, free to love others the way they should be loved because he isn't "self" conscious. He's not so hung up on himself that he has to continually make his point or prove himself.

Does he have a vision for his life and a job? A man needs to feel good about himself and be productive before he should even think about committing to a relationship. It's no coincidence that Ruth met Boaz in the field during harvest season and Rebekah first saw Isaac standing in a field. There is significance to a man being in full swing of doing his thing that makes him ready to cover the woman in his life. He is wired by God to know he should protect and provide for her. He knows his wife was entrusted into his care by God. A godly husband wants to live up to his God-given mandate to do the right thing. He might not be a millionaire, but he is wealthy in the Lord's love and purpose.

Mr. Right is a man who serves God and has a character consistent with the Bible's description of the fruit of the Holy Spirit. He exhibits "love, joy, peace, forbearance [patience], kindness, goodness, faithfulness, gentleness and self-control" (Galatians 5:22-23). He is not selfish or self-seeking. He is all of that and a bag of chips! He is honest, keeps his promises, wants to be transparent, and is loyal. He loves you and he speaks of forever with you.

And last, this man is to be a *complement* to your life. He *adds* to you as a person. He encourages you to become a better woman. He makes sure you feel secure. Your relationship together improves your relationship with God. It also improves your relationships with others. If your man's presence in your life places you in conflict with God, people, or yourself, he is not the one for you! His presence should add love, joy, and peace to your life. And that peace factor is huge. If you're constantly doubting his love for you or finding your self-esteem plummeting when you're around him, you need to evaluate if he's the best choice for you.

Your partner should add new, positive dimensions to your life. He should encourage your spiritual growth. Your life should be better than it was before he came into your life. And some of these improvements should be obvious to the people around you too. That is the witness that yes, your relationship is a good thing for both of you.

I need to step in here with a reality check. Some men seem to exhibit all these great qualities, so women fall in love with them...but the relationships don't progress. Here is where a woman can turn left when she should go right. She keeps dating that man hoping, wishing, praying that one day a light will come on in his head and he will say, "Let's get married!" But that's not realistic. I'm sure there were indicators long before she finally got the clue that he wasn't going to marry her. Friend, if your man's major plans are all about him and don't include you, look out. If he's buying cars and planning long-term goals without your input, don't ignore that check in your spirit. If he's settled into a comfortable place with you and isn't in need of anything other than what you're already giving him, you will be his long-term girlfriend and not his wife.

Dear Michelle,

I've been dating the same guy for six years. I know he is the one for me because he's everything I've ever wanted. He's handsome and successful. We have amazing chemistry, and we like the same things. I've given him everything, but every time I approach the subject of where the relationship is going, he gets defensive. I don't understand it. Our relationship is so perfect. Why wouldn't he want to seal our commitment?

He does have a bit of a temper, and my mother thinks he needs anger management classes. But he only gets like that when he's stressed out.

I really love him, and I can't imagine spending the rest of my life with anyone else. I feel he is my Mr. Right, but I'm beginning to wonder if I'm wrong...

Waiting in Vain

Dear Waiting in Vain,

Perhaps you could use an ego boost so you realize you deserve more. When a man really loves a woman, he thinks of little else. He puts her first. He wants to do more than be with her; he wants to claim her for his own.

You say you've given him everything, so it's safe to assume you've probably granted him all the privileges of a husband by now. In that case, he may not feel he has to actually become one. But the other part of the equation is that you've listed nothing but shallow and changeable qualities as the reasons you love this man. Then on top of all of that you mention he has anger issues. He sounds like Mr. Wrong to me. But perhaps I need to go deeper. What do you think he's right for?

Obviously even he knows he isn't fit for a lasting commitment. Girl, your Mr. Right will be an intentional man who wants to commit. He will recognize your value and want to claim you as his own. Once he does that, he'll want to protect you and provide for you as his investment. And when you believe that's what you deserve, you won't settle for less. Perhaps the man is actually doing you a favor by not popping the question. Thank God for giving you time to come to your senses, and then move on. The one thing a good woman can't afford to do is waste time!

If he sounds wrong and acts
wrong, he's just wrong.
Michelle

Keeping It Real

Remember Adam naming all those animals in the garden? He recognized that not one of them was a good match for him. They were perfectly suited for the one created after its own kind, but not for him. My mother used to say, "There's an owner for every cloth in the store."

I also like this related saying: "One man's trash is another man's treasure." That's so true! Every man you meet is right for somebody—he just may not be right for you. This is why you need to be in touch with your needs and desires and be sensitive to God's leading. He knows what you need more than you do.

"Mr. Right" might not be obvious to your eye at first, but with time and information who he will be in your life will become clearer to your heart and spirit as you move forward. When you limit yourself to a specific type when considering potential mates, you might be blocking out God's choice for you! The "type" you normally like might be the essence of what fantasies are made of, but he won't wear well in reality. The Mr. Right God brings to you might not be so colorful, but he will be very solid. He might not be really exciting, but he will be faithful. Are you getting where I'm taking you? Get realistic about what it takes to make long-lasting relationships work. When your desires and focus change, the men you let into your life will change too.

Are you wondering if there is just one person for you or whether you should have many men around you so your options are more open? My answer is there are many men you could marry and live with rather comfortably, but I believe one specific man will ultimately be Mr. Best for you.

Also make sure you pray and listen so you'll hear what God's direction is. Don't over spiritualize. Be prayerful and seek God for confirmation on whether you're moving in the right direction. Also pay attention to natural details as well as the other factors we've been discussing. As one of my mentors instructed me, "You must like the person, love the person, and be 'in love' with the person, along with being spiritually at peace." Remember, scripturally speaking, it is first natural attraction that draws two people together, and then, if they decide they've met their perfect match, they marry and their spirits are knit together to form a spiritual and physical bond, thus the two become one.

When you find the man of your dreams, no one's opinion will really matter except God's and yours. Mr. Right might not be right to anyone else's eyes, but he will be perfect to yours.

13

The Question Is...

Ah, yes, at some point questions must be asked. So you've met this amazing man. He's wonderful. He makes you feel beautiful, intelligent, and so on. The conversations are deep and fascinating. The chemistry is at the boiling point. Everything seems to be moving in the right direction—but how do you really know?

One day I got on a bus. It was a pleasant ride with beautiful scenery. Rather enjoyable, I must say. But after riding for about an hour, I realized nothing looked familiar. I discovered I'd been going in the wrong direction! I was completely opposite to where I really wanted to go. I was lost, behind schedule, and had to backtrack. I lost a lot of productive time because it was taking twice the allotted time to reach my desired destination. Get the picture?

Though relationships take time to build, one danger is spending too much time on something that isn't going anywhere. So how do you know if you're heading toward the altar or the playground? When is the right time to ask the critical, hard questions that must be asked? God does make everything beautiful in its time, but two people can mar the beauty that was intended by not engaging their minds along with their hearts. There is a reason the Bible says to "watch over your heart with all diligence, for from it flow the springs of life" (Proverbs 4:23 NASB).

Often disappointment is when you make an appointment the other party doesn't keep. Being on the lonely end of a "dissed" appointment can throw your heart, mind, and spirit into chaos. I believe most heartbreak is totally unnecessary. Though love requires risk, far too many take excessive risks. Where is the balance between accepting the risk of romance and utilizing wisdom to avoid it? It is a delicate dance.

Many people are afraid to ask serious questions about their relationships because they feel asking questions will scare the other person away. I say that if questions scare them away, they were going away anyway. I believe it's better to find out information sooner than later. An intentional man will gladly answer your questions because it solidifies in his mind that you are also emotionally invested. Your questions free him to accept what he's feeling and share his thoughts without fear of being rejected.

And listening is just as important as asking questions. A lot of your questions might even be answered *before* you ask. For instance, if a man is talking about the future and it sounds as if no one else significant is included, then you know you're not part of his big picture yet. Listen for the switch from "I" to "we." Remember that timing is everything. Ask questions too soon and you can short circuit the positive progression of emotions. There is no need to ask his intentions on a first date because he probably doesn't know. You can ask him if he's in another relationship. That's an important issue that sets the stage for how you deal with his approach and attention. His answer will let you know if he goes in the "potential mate file," the "friendship file," or the "never see again file." (Although potential mates should begin as friends, I'm specifically talking about seeing the big picture here.)

Intentions can't be solidified when you don't have enough information to draw clear conclusions. This is why I say "dating is not for mating; it is for collecting data." Free-flowing conversations provide more unsolicited data than you could ever hope to gather from an interview. In an interview-type situation, the person may provide false information because he wants to please you and say what you want to hear. But when there is no conscious examination, all filters are turned off. And that is what you want—an unedited script on how this person feels about you and where he wants the relationship to go.

Before you ask him questions about how you fit into his life, you need to know what his plans for his life are. You might not want to be part of them after you find out. Far too many people go forward on chemistry alone, leaving purpose and vision out of their decision to pursue the relationship. Later, after they get together and the fireworks die down a bit, they discover they don't have the same vision for the future. The phrase "we outgrew one another" isn't really accurate. The two people weren't in the same place with the same vision to begin with.

I recommend beginning by casually asking general life questions, including:

- Where do you see yourself in a year? Where do you see yourself in five years?
- What is important to you?
- What is your picture of an ideal romantic relationship?
- Do you think you'll get married someday?
- Do you want children?

Yes, for all you know he might be happy being single, being a confirmed bachelor. If he is and you want to be married, then this man isn't the one for you. And here is where you must implement an important piece of advice: *Whatever the man says, believe him.* Don't make the mistake of thinking you can change his mind. That is not your job. Your job is to discern the truth based on his words and actions. The truth may hurt at first, but it does set you free to move on.

When do you ask more personal questions? Questions about you and him and where the relationship is going? When he's shown he's interested in you romantically. You then have the right to bring it up! God's Word clearly tells us not to stir up love until it's time (Song of

Songs 2:7). If the man is making romantic moves toward you, such as touching and kissing, you can ask as many questions as you want to. Anytime a man moves into your personal space, you're entitled to ask what he intends to do with that space now and for the long term. After all, it is *your* space—your heart, your emotions, your mind, your spirit. You are the keeper and protector of these very important aspects of yourself. It behooves you to be a good steward and gatekeeper. To ask relationship questions before he's indicated he's interested romantically would be premature and might make you seem presumptuous. No sense in putting him on the defensive; simply wait until you have a solid basis for asking your questions. Until then guard your heart and gather enough information to ask the right questions.

Dear Michelle,

I'm trying to figure out exactly where I am in my relationship with my guy. He has never officially said that we are in a relationship, but he blows up my phone night and day, always wanting to know where I am. We've never had "the talk" though. This relationship has been going on for over a year, and I still don't know where we are. Is it possible to just organically grow into a relationship? We are together all the time. I'm not seeing anyone else, and he never talks about anyone else. Is it safe for me to assume we are a couple?

Please help me understand.

I'm Just Saying...

Dear Just Saying,

It would be better if I knew exactly what you're saying. My mother used to tell me that when I "assume" things, I can take that word apart to see what I would become. Assuming makes a donkey (I'll say it nicely) out of "u" and "me." Don't you want to know sooner rather than later where you are with this man? How much of yourself do you want to invest before you discover you're getting no return out of the deal? I believe that's like throwing money at a blind investment only to find out later it was fake stock. All your money is gone, and you've gotten nothing back for it.

Your heart is a terrible thing to waste, girlfriend. The thing you need to know is that a man seldom does anything he doesn't have to in a relationship. If you are allowing him to "float on" as the old song says, you might end up watching your relationship fade into the sunset. Anyone who gets in a car, taxi, bus, train, or plane knows where she is going. You owe it to your heart to know where you're being taken—just for a ride or toward a real destination.

No man should be allowed to constantly blow up your phone with calls and text messages unless he's committed to you, unless he's all in on your relationship. Otherwise he's taking up space and getting in the way of someone who might be willing to commit. It's not fair to you to allow him to take you off the market without making his intentions known. He needs to know your love isn't free. That you aren't giving your heart away. True love costs you everything, so don't allow anyone to take it for granted because he is too lazy or selfish to make a commitment.

Men who don't make it clear about where they are in relationship with their women are still shopping. Your man is keeping his options open while robbing you of yours. So the next time boyfriend lights up your phone wondering where you are, you need to find out why he wants to know—if you get what I mean.

You didn't mention if he has introduced you to his friends and family. This is huge! If all your time with him is spent as a *"coo-some twosome," you are being kept in the dark for a reason you may not like. Men like to show off their trophies when they're fully invested in winning them.*

Okay, this is critical. Repeat after me: "I have no more time to waste on a relationship that isn't going anywhere. I have no more time to waste on a relationship that isn't going anywhere." Now repeat that one more time for good measure. Then continue with, "I will ask the hard questions because I have a right to know where this relationship is going. Then I will be walking in the truth because it sets me free." Now believe it!

Michelle

Keeping It Real

What a man doesn't say is just as important as what he does say, so listen to both forms. Never apologize for asking questions. You deserve to know where the relationship is going. Here's a simple rule to remember: If your man won't tell you that you're in a relationship, the only thing you can really know is that *you aren't in one*. Most men are very territorial. They like to claim things and mark their territory—whether it's a plot of land or a woman. Trust me on this. When they want to own something, they claim it. If you haven't been claimed, feel free to stay in the marketplace, being open to any options that come your way. Don't let a noncommittal man block you from being viewed by someone who will have the courage and passion to see you for the prize you are and want to claim you.

And perhaps that's the real issue. Do you see yourself as the prize you are? If so, make it clear you expect to be treated as a precious, desirable woman. If you're unsure of your worth, remember you are a child of the King of kings! Don't apologize for being so valuable! Your man should know your true worth and act accordingly!

14

Setting Boundaries

Now that I live in Africa and travel quite a bit, one of the most prominent things I've noticed is the difference between roads with curbs and sidewalks and those that have no boundaries and just fade into whatever is on either side of it. These are the places where refuse and other various and sundry things are also found. Litter prevails. But where there are curbs and sidewalks, it is clean and orderly. Yes, boundaries help create order. Boundaries help create safety. Everyone knows where the boundaries are so they know where they should be. Usually they stay within the confines of the limits that have been set, and this keeps everyone moving forward in safety. Without the lines in the streets, chaos would reign because everyone would be driving hither, thither, and yon, ultimately crashing because everyone went his or her own way.

Relationships need boundaries too. They need lines that will not be crossed. If these don't exist, people can get hurt. Setting boundaries that require both of you to own your part in the relationship and the issues that arise is not only healthy but strengthens the relationship in the long run. Sometimes in an effort not to rock the boat in a relationship, no one takes the time to agree to what the acceptable limitations should be. For example, faithfulness is a good boundary to set. If you're in a committed relationship, faithfulness is a boundary you should insist on if you've both agreed you care for one another enough to move forward together. Sharing your man with another person romantically is not acceptable to you. You certainly don't want to discover he has one or more women besides you in his life. And I'm sure he feels the same about you and other men. Faithfulness, my friend, should be a *serious* boundary!

There are other critical boundaries that set precedents for respect, honor, and love in your relationship, including time, physical body, physical space, psychological matters, and sexuality.

Time. Your time should never be taken for granted. Until you're married, no man should feel entitled to drop by your house anytime day or night without calling first and considering your schedule. If he does, that reveals attitudes of selfishness and, perhaps, insecurity and inconsideration. A person who is caring and loves you will always consider your time. He will not take it for granted that he is the only component of your life that matters. He will not assume he is a primary pillar of your life. He knows your time is valuable and appreciates that you are willing to share it with him. And you do the same for him. Neither of you makes plans that include the other person without checking to make sure it fits with both of your schedules and desires. Both of you need to be free to spend time with others or on pursuits other than the relationship.

Physical body. Another boundary that is critical to set is your body. Any kind of physical abuse is a *huge* red flag. In fact, your policy needs to be simple and to the point. Abuse will not be tolerated. Once signs of potential physical abuse appear or outright assault occurs, don't stay in the relationship! This is a character issue in the abuser. If he hits you once, he will certainly hit you again no matter how sorry he says he is afterward. Believe it whether you want to or not. Abusers try to make you believe the assault was your fault—that you did something to deserve it. He's wrong. If he hits you, the abuse is his fault regardless of the circumstances. It is his fault for not resolving the conflict or expressing himself in a nondestructive fashion. Send the message loud and clear that you are not someone who will tolerate abuse in any form. No one deserves that sort of treatment. Absolutely no one.

Physical space (residential). This one is short, sweet, and simple to take care of. Your house should remain your house until you are married. Fact: Many couples who live together never marry. And those who do marry usually end up unhappy or divorced. According to National Health Statistics Reports, March 22, 2012, "It has been well documented that women and men who cohabit with their future spouse before first marriage are more likely to divorce than those who do not cohabit with their spouse before first marriage." My mama put it this way: "Why buy the cow if you can get the milk for free?" I agree by saying, "Don't be a wife until you *are* a wife."

Another negative about living together before marriage is that you have no legal rights if something happens to your man. I know of cases where the man died and his children from a former marriage took possession of everything and kicked the "lover" out.

Psychological. No one should play detrimental or demeaning mind games with you. If you get a clue that is happening, shut it down right away. Mental abuse is just as prevalent as physical abuse and far more subtle. Manipulating you into believing that everything wrong in the relationship is your fault is not acceptable behavior. Putting you down and disrespecting your personhood in any way is abuse. In a true love relationship, each person considers the other as important as him- or herself. Both people strive to achieve comfort and security on all levels for each other. Mutually submitting to each other leaves no room for making one partner feel bad or questioning his or her worth. Both of you should be strengthened and encouraged by each other.

Sexual. We live in a no-holds-barred world where it seems that sexually all limits are off. Yet God's Word clearly sets boundaries for our physical desires and inclinations. His basic rule is no sex outside of marriage. (I'm sure I just heard an audible groan.) And yet if we were all honest, we would say that this is the area that wreaks the most havoc in relationships. When women cross this boundary, the shame, the pain, the angst over whether those men appreciated the fact that they were given this privilege has caused many a woman to sob deeply and experience depression and low self-esteem. How many have lived in regret and suffered consequences for misusing the gift of sexual intimacy? For some, deep scars remain physically, emotionally, and spiritually. I'm convinced that those who break up after experiencing sexual intimacy with their partners weep more over the parts of themselves they can never take back than they do the physical departure of the man.

Yet it is important to remember that we were created for intimacy with God and with our life partner. God wired us to crave these connections. As with all our God-given desires, they are lawful but not beneficial if they aren't applied at the right time and in the right manner. You both will need to covenant with each other to honor God and each other through abstinence until you're married.

Sex before marriage is like allowing a child to grow up too soon. What does he have to look forward to if he does everything by the age of 13? Where does he go from there? Could this be part of the problem with marriages today? The search for a greater thrill extends beyond the marriage because all the thrill cards got used up before you said "I do"? Remember the words of Potiphar's wife to the slave Joseph: "Lie with me" (Genesis 39:7). Never a truer sentence has been spoken! Intimacy without commitment is a lie, and kisses are definitely not a promise of anything beyond that moment. Both include no guarantee of "to have and to hold forever."

Dear Michelle,

I've been dating the same man for quite a few years. It's been a relationship made for Lifetime TV. I've busted him with several women. He's always so mortified, apologizes profusely, and does anything and everything to win me back.

He refuses to marry me. I'm emotionally spent at this

point. I don't understand him. He has no complaints about me. I do everything for him. I'm faithful. I'm not a nagger. And yet it seems that my friends around me who are much more demanding and crazy end up getting married while I remain a bridesmaid.

Never the Bride

Dear Never,

At the rate you're going, your prediction will hold true. The difference between you and your demanding gal pals is they've set boundaries. I'm going to turn to a verse in the book of Proverbs that may, at first, seem like an odd choice. "Foolishness is bound up in the heart of a child; the rod of discipline will remove it far from him." Why that Scripture you ask? Because of the principle behind it. The man you're dating is a "man child." You should not be his mother! You must set boundaries that will help set the course of your relationship toward the goal you desire. You want respect, honor, and love. If you have those three things along with desire, you will probably end up married because the man who provides those things will want to put you in a good light for all who surround you to see. The best way he can respect, honor, and love you is to give you his name. That's the ultimate sign of his honor.

If you continue to allow your man to run rampant over you, he'll keep on stepping because there's nothing to rein him in. Setting boundaries doesn't have to be done in a manner that is intimidating or unattractive. Who you are should have made a statement about your boundaries, so now you need to provide some boundary guidance.

However, in your case, I think you've probably gone well past the boundaries that should have been set from the beginning. Your man refuses to marry you? Then why are you still with him? He has made his intentions clear. If you never want to get married and just want an uncommitted companion remain with him. He's been unfaithful, not once but several times! Then he obviously isn't remorseful enough to stop the behavior. True repentance involves asking God for forgiveness and help, turning away from repeating the offense, and taking steps to make sure it never happens again.

I say this man has used up all his boundary coupons, whether you laid them out clearly or not. Some things go without being said if you truly love someone, and fidelity is one of them.

Girl, you've made life way too convenient and easy for this "man-child" or selfish manipulator. You need to stop believing that something is better than nothing! Drop kick this guy to the curb and keep on stepping. Don't waste another second by remaining with this guy.

So it's time to take a deep breath and throw down the gauntlet. If you want to get married, you need to tell him goodbye. Talk to God, pack your bags, and find someone who knows your true worth and will love you so much he'll want you all to himself.

This man showed you who he was—unfaithful and selfish. He did you a favor by not asking you to marry him. Now free yourself to get what you truly deserve—a man who knows what he wants, knows a good woman when he sees you, and knows what he wants enough to make the commitment to loving you.

Here's to drawing lines in the sand,
Michelle

Keeping It Real

Repeat after me: "Boundaries are good!" They are good for you, and they are good for your partner. They keep everyone clear on where you are and where you're going. Street signs let you know where to turn. There is no need to turn if the street doesn't lead to where you want to go. If you don't want a lasting commitment, you don't have to pay attention to anything I've said. You can sit back and let the relationship run its course until it fades to black because, believe me, it will. Or you can move on, and when you find a man who truly appreciates you and wants to find out more, this time set the necessary boundaries. Where do you want to go in this new relationship? If you want your relationship to go the distance and last, you must keep that destination in mind as you move forward.

Now, even in a committed relationship your man can veer off course a bit. In that case, have *gentle* conversations with him that will help him turn to the paths you've both decided upon. You can say something like, "I need you to help me feel better about our relationship by..." and finish with what you want him to do or don't want him to do. Keep it simple. No screaming, no raging, no arguing. Just give a statement of the facts regarding the error and what you need from him at this point.

Men are fixers! Hopefully your guy will follow through since he now has specific goals or steps to solve the problem. Without guidance on the relationship and your expectations, he may drift on to someone willing to be more specific. So woman up! Put your foot down firmly but gently and set boundaries. They create order and clear the road for forward movement.

15

The Big "V"

I felt as if someone had socked me in the stomach. I was relating my latest romance trauma to one of my spiritual mothers. When I finished, she was silent for a moment before saying something that rocked my world:

> Michelle, I have watched you for a long time. I've been privy to most of the relationships you've had. I've noticed you do the same thing in every one. You never give the man a safe place to land. He never feels safe with you. And you must understand that for a man to ask you the question you want to hear, you must help him feel safe enough to ask it. He needs to know you will say yes.

Well, you could have knocked me over with a feather. I pushed the replay button on my relationships, and as I recalled the events of each one, I realized she was right. In fact, many of the men had told me what she'd said but in different ways. I recalled asking one of my ex-boyfriends (several years after recovering from my broken heart) why he'd never asked me to marry him. He calmly replied, "Because you never asked me to!" I was taken aback. After all, wasn't he the one who was supposed to propose? And yet I've heard so many times that the woman is the one who is really in control when it comes to romantic relationships. (Though we might contest that fact since men are supposed to be the pursuers.) So what was I to learn from this information? That my capacity to be vulnerable has a great deal to do with how successful my relationships are and where they will ultimately end up.

Yes, "vulnerable" is the big "V." Wait a sec! Don't put the book down and leave the room! I promise—vulnerability isn't that bad even though it does require great strength. Does that sound like an oxymoron? It isn't. Pride is the antithesis of vulnerability, and so often we use it as a cover because we're afraid to be real. To be exposed. To be naked emotionally. And yet the very first relationship began with two people being naked, hiding nothing until sin entered into the picture and they both ran for cover.

I always prided myself on not being reactionary in my love relationships. I was calm and controlled until the situation reached a point I didn't like. That's when I packed my emotional bags and moved to another country. Have you heard the saying "Drop it like it's hot"? I was the master of that—kicking the man to the curb and never looking back. And, of course, my actions didn't do anything to diminish the devastation I felt when he didn't come after me or when he eventually married someone else. At some point I sort of noticed that the women who leaned on their men, who were honest about their emotions, and who let them know they were needed seemed to get their marriage dreams fulfilled.

Do you get the idea that being vulnerable was something I needed to study and come to grips with? I turned to my favorite book, the Bible, for some answers. First I looked to Jesus. He was vulnerable to the point of death to get His bride (the church, including you and me!). He was willing to be humble and authentic. Oh, how we need to follow His example! We need to be real with how we're feeling and what our needs and wants are. The enemy of our souls does such a good job of encouraging us to assume what's going on with the other person instead of being vulnerable enough to ask. Between the fear of knowing and the assumptions we make, our failure to be open can decimate any relationship. What heart can stand against all that? Ours! Here's the secret. Just as "meekness" can be defined as "power under control," vulnerability can be viewed as giving the men in our lives permission and inspiration to be the men God wants them to be.

Our men want to be our heroes. They live for this! And if we want heroes, we have to be vulnerable so they know what they need to do. There is no shame in revealing vulnerability.

The Nitty-Gritty

Now, girl, I'm not talking about going crazy, manipulating your man all over the place or overplaying your hand. Vulnerability is really about laying everything down—all weapons of war, all pretenses, all pride, and all that might impede the flow of love. Remember, truth sets everybody free, so shame the devil by keeping it real. If you're hurting, say so. Now don't say it in anger or with an accusatory tone. Be authentic. Tell him how you're feeling and what you need from him to help you feel better about the relationship.

Your man will be very appreciative of instruction when it comes to helping you. He wants the manual on what you need. He can't always figure it out, which makes him confused and frustrated. And a frustrated man might handle the situation by acting like a child or bully, depending on his insecurities. Bullies try to exert power over you to make you feel lesser so they'll feel better about themselves. Children will reach for instant gratification of some kind.

Depending on how badly you want your man, you need to swallow your pride and let him know what you need from him. And while you're at it, ask him what he needs from you! Let this conversation be an "equal opportunity talk" designed to bring you closer. When he feels safe and not threatened, he'll open up to you. And when you show him the part of you that is soft and tender and needs his protection, he will man up to the occasion.

Remember, God wired him to cover and protect his woman. It's built into him to respond to your needs when you let him see them. Pride and posturing on your part calls up a different attitude in him—resistance and war! So speak from your heart. Keep it real and free of anger and facades. Then watch your man buckle on his sword and head out to slay whatever is threatening you!

Dear Michelle,

I find myself in a rather deep dilemma. Where is the balance point between being transparent with your man and being a downright fool? I don't want my kindness to be considered a weakness or an act of desperation. When does being nicey-nicey end because he's continuing to do the things I don't like?

One of my friends is always crying and whining to her man, and I'm like, "Puh-leeze!" I'm just not that kind of person. I'd rather be alone before I go through any gyrations of helplessness just to feed a man's ego.

The last man in my life thought it was okay to have a girlfriend while he figured out if he wanted to be with me or not. I helped him make his decision by kicking him out of my life. I don't have time for that nonsense. Why can't men just make up their minds? I'll tell you why—because they don't have to! Are they all players? I think so, and here is one woman who refuses to be played.

As for vulnerability, don't you have to wait until you find a man who is worth being vulnerable to, who proves he's safe enough to hear all your stuff? And how will I know when I've found him?

Help!
Too Many Questions

Dear Questions,

Whew! There's a lot going on in your letter. I don't think you have too many questions, girl. I think you have too much anger. While it is true that he wasn't worthy of your time and attention and you did the right thing by letting him go, you shouldn't let your past hurts interfere with or ruin future relationships. It's hard to be vulnerable when you're that ticked off! Vulnerability isn't about manipulating someone to get the results you want. It's about achieving the liberty that comes when you can be yourself, when you can be authentic. Being able to admit what you're feeling so you don't have to be defensive or angry is actually empowering. It frees you from negativity.

When you keep it real with your man, it's on him to choose to respond appropriately. That is not your weight to carry. If you decide you didn't get the results you wanted and decide to walk, at least you can leave like a lady, knowing you gave it your best shot. You gave him enough rope to hang himself. If you walk away without being your authentic self and expressing everything you wanted him to know, you will always live with the discomfort of not having been honest. You'll wonder if you coulda, woulda, shoulda. The devil will use your lack of vulnerability against you. He will torture you with all sorts of different scenarios after the fact. You'll live with unnecessary regrets. Trust me on this. I've been there, done that several times. Jesus said, "No one takes [my life] from me, but I lay it down of my own accord. I have authority to lay it down and authority to take it up again" (John 10:17). That is the power of vulnerability. No one can take anything from you unless you choose to give it. Being vulnerable doesn't make you a fool. On the contrary, it reveals you are a strong, powerful woman who is brave enough to be authentic.

As for your question about the man in your life...you are in control. If you want to, you can be his friend while he's deciding about the relationship. Just don't include any girlfriend benefits until he makes up his mind. If you think your heart will be in trouble by remaining his friend while he makes up his mind, be open and honest. Tell him your heart can't deal with sharing him so you're going to back off on the relationship until he decides who he really wants to be with. Do you see what's happening? You are choosing what will happen based on what you know about yourself and your heart condition.

In the meantime, let off some of that steam by releasing your pain and anger to God. Talk to Him. Ask Him to heal you so you will be free to be someone who freely shares her heart even knowing the cost. Loving authentically may cost you dearly, but you will gain more than you'll ever be able to give. That's the way love works. It multiplies when you give it away.

Move forward softly.
Michelle

Keeping It Real

If you're thinking about the effect your transparency will have on your man, you're not operating in the right spirit. Anger is unyielded rights. Do you have the right to have a committed relationship that is free from unfaithfulness? Yes, you do. Absolutely. But don't let past disappointment from bad relationships create a shell around your heart that makes it difficult to be real when you meet a man who is trustworthy and deserving. Too many women harbor so much anger that they systematically sabotage every relationship they have. They view the repeated pain as justification to hold onto bitterness that continues to grow and invite more of the same. Clinging to the right to protect yourself can help you protect yourself right out of a relationship you want.

When it comes to intimate relationships, you need to refuse to cling to your rights. They so easily become demands you make on your man, and he may not be able to meet them every time. When you stop expecting divinity from your very human partner, you release him to be who he really is. At the same time, you release yourself to be transparent about what your needs are. Authenticity is crucial to every relationship. No one loses in this process, and it always feels good to be honest and get things off your chest. This diffuses anger and keeps bitterness from building up. It also sets the atmosphere for both of you to share from your hearts and gain a better understanding of each other. No wonder God's Word encourages people to get wisdom and understanding!

> Do not let wisdom and understanding out of your sight,
> preserve sound judgment and discretion;
> they will be life for you,
> an ornament to grace your neck.
> Then you will go on your way in safety,
> and your foot will not stumble.
> When you lie down, you will not be afraid;
> when you lie down, your sleep will be sweet
> (Proverbs 3:21-24).

Wisdom and discretion will guide you on what to say, when to say it, and how to say it to nurture a fruitful exchange. Understanding gives you and your partner the wisdom you need to meet each other's needs to the best of your abilities and flourish in your relationship. "The fear of the LORD is the beginning of wisdom, and knowledge of the Holy One is understanding" (Proverbs 9:10). You were created to love and be loved tenderly, gently, authentically.

16

Sex

Ah, sex. Now that I have your attention, let's tackle this hot topic that seems to constantly be on the minds and hearts of most of mankind. I'm going to take my time on this because I believe that even though sexuality is discussed over and over in and out of the church, a lot of misinformation is creating turmoil as singles (and some married people) struggle while navigating the delicate dance between obeying the Word of God and handling their very real physical and emotional desires. And, girl, if you've already messed up a few of the dance steps, don't despair. "If we confess our sins, he is faithful and just to forgive us our sins and to cleanse us from all unrighteousness" (1 John 1:9 ESV).

I was speaking with a friend of mine who had simply accepted the fact that he couldn't refrain from engaging in sex outside of marriage. He said he got so tired of falling into this sin trap and then repenting that he just decided this would be a weakness he'd just learn to live with. Even though this man absolutely loves the Lord, when it came to sex, he imploded from frustration. The flipside of my friend's decision is that he may never experience an urgency to select a mate because his physical and emotional needs are already being fulfilled.

Are you involved sexually with your boyfriend? As my mentor P.B. Wilson says, the release of testosterone in a man's system every 48 to 72 hours is a wake-up call for him to find a mate. When his desires are satisfied, he figuratively goes to sleep. So if you're wondering why your man isn't waking up and smelling the coffee, it could be because you keep putting him to sleep by engaging in premarital sex with him. You are killing his need to commit to you.

As you get more and more comfortable being sexually active with your partner, you run the danger of becoming calloused to sin and hard-of-hearing when the Holy Spirit is communicating with you. God will not force you to obey His Word. He will let you indulge in your inclinations if you insist, but you will suffer the consequences of violating His standards.

Though fear of the Lord is the beginning of wisdom, I believe that walking in purity can't be sustained if your choice is based on fear of punishment or retribution alone. If you try to obey God based on fear alone, you won't succeed and, eventually, you'll become resentful and angry. The decisions you make regarding following God and living according to His Word must be made out of your sincere love for Him...out of your personal and intimate relationship with Him.

Okay, I hear you! "I love God, so why is it such a struggle to sustain sexual purity?" The answer is simple: God created you with the desire for intimacy. You were created to be intimate with Him and have the desire for emotional and sexual intimacy with your husband (if you marry) for closeness and procreation. The reality in the world today is that as people are waiting longer and longer to marry the struggle to refrain from sex before marriage is escalated. Back in the day, people got married early, in their teens as a matter of fact. Literally you went from your parents' house to your mate's house. There was no long respite between leaving your parents' house and marriage. A woman went straight from living a sheltered existence with a high degree of accountability and an emphasis on sexual purity to being married, so it was easier to stay pure that's for sure. Of course, sexual temptation has always been alive and well from the beginning of time after the fall, à la David and Bathsheba, Amnon and Tamar, and Samson and Delilah. But for the most part Jewish society in biblical times made much less provision for sexual promiscuity than where we are presently.

It seemed the only notes we get in the Bible on people stepping out of order are extremes, including rape, incest, and intermarriage with people who practice pagan religions. But now we're seeing an onslaught of media on the fact that folks are saved, single, and engaging in sex despite God's disapproval. I believe the decline in Christian morality is due to the fact that, first, most people have no idea of God's view of sex, and second, that we're basically not adhering to God's original design to be married much earlier in life. People were created to desire intimate relationships. For most of us, it goes against the grain of how we were created to reach mid adulthood—our thirties, forties, and above—without being committed to a romantic relationship and experiencing intimacy.

Back in biblical times, people lived a lot longer so the cycles of life probably also took longer to play out. Sarah didn't have a child until she was 99, but I'm sure she was intimate with her husband long before that. With the exception of those who have the "gift" of singleness and choose to live celibate lives, the rest of us struggle to deal with our very real physical and emotional desires while obeying God's Word. At times, depending on age, hormonal factors, and so forth, the physical struggle can seem overwhelming. This is a physiological fact. The body needs a release. Sexual intimacy is not just productive, as in producing children, or binding, as in two people committed to each other, it is also rejuvenating. It releases chemicals in the body that help it revitalize. Sex within marriage is good for you!

"What about Jesus?" you ask. He was in His thirties and single. The apostle Paul was also single and up there in age. What about him? These men were sold out to a single cause—to promoting the kingdom of God. They had a deeply personal and intimate relationship with God and were completely consumed with purpose. Did they deal with sexual desire? I'm sure they did, but they mastered their bodies and thought lives. They redirected their passions into sharing God and the gospel. This is one reason Paul was so adamant about keeping the body in control, comparing it to a runner who has mastered the discipline to stay in shape and win the race. He also stressed corralling your thought life, keeping it in line with God's principles.

Although we too should be focused on sharing Christ, unfortunately this is not where most people live today. It's also safe to say that most haven't been called by God to live that type of life. We're called to a life of surrender to Christ, yes, but not all are called to give their lives completely to ministry. I believe this is why Paul called singleness a gift:

> I wish that all of you were as I am. But each of you has your own gift from God; one has this gift, another has that. Now to the unmarried and the widows I say: It is good for them to stay unmarried, as I do. But if they cannot control themselves, they should marry, for it is better to marry than to burn with passion (1 Corinthians 7:7-9).

He knew and understood everyone wasn't cut out for his lifestyle, so he recommended marriage to accommodate the natural desires God placed inside us. I'm not putting anyone under condemnation. If you've committed sexual sin, repent and ask for God's forgiveness. He will grant it! And determine to follow God's principles from this point forward with God's help. God knows we are sinners. The more we grow in our love for Him, the more we'll want to please Him instead of grieving His heart with our disobedience.

Why does sexual sin seem like not a big deal anymore? Why don't we understand the depth of sexual sin? Because we don't see (or refuse to see) or understand the spiritual component. Sex isn't just a physical act. It engages the emotions and makes us one with another human being. Sex is also a spiritual act of worship. I often use an unusual analogy to explain this concept. I'm sure you know many heathen religions included sexual activity in their temples and for other rites. They had temple prostitutes who performed all sorts of sexual acts with the worshippers as tributes to their various gods. I believe there is a spiritual component in human sexuality that bears fruit within marriage. Imagine that the woman's body is the holy of holies and the man is the high priest. When he enters the holy of holies, he must come bearing no offense or sin. It was a matter of life and death (Exodus 28:35; Leviticus 16:2). This is why Paul said that to present our bodies as a living sacrifice is our reasonable act of worship (Romans 12:1). He wanted to direct us away from fleshly practices and toward the spiritual act of worshipping God. He presented controlling our sexuality before marriage as a way to surrender our all to God, as a way to worship Him as we walk in obedience to Him. What is sex? What is worship? They are both the act of giving all you are to the one you love, an act of surrender of giving up yourself.

One of the Greek words for "worship" in the New Testament can be translated "kiss forward," signifying an intimate exchange with God. Not in the sexual sense, but in coming to Him and pouring out your love with no sin, no offense, standing between Him and you. When we surrender in obedience to God, we become one with Him. Jesus said that He and His Father were one (John 10:30). When you see or know Him, you see and know the Father (John 14:9). Jesus did nothing apart from His Father (John 8:28-29). As we grow in oneness with God, we become more and more like Him. That is how we glorify Him—by being a reflection of His love and attributes in human form.

After you marry, God will bless your union and the physical exchange of love between you and your spouse because you are in covenant. Husband and wife surrender to one another, which births a deeper level of knowing one another, of becoming one. Intimacy births revelation, and revelation brings about transformation in our lives. The longer two people are married to each other, the more they seem like one in many ways. They even begin to look alike! This comes from the deep intimacy they share spiritually, emotionally, and sexually.

Yes, sex is a very powerful union that binds two people together. It should not be taken lightly.

Back to the Garden?

I like comparing married love and lovemaking to returning to the Garden of Eden. Once again man and woman are naked and unashamed. To achieve that, the man and the woman need to be within the safety net of a lasting covenant—a marriage covenant. In the same vein, I compare engaging in sex outside of marriage to leaving the Garden of Eden, simply implying that the loss of purity that brings security and trust to the relationship has been sacrificed when intimacy takes place outside of covenant.

I was talking with some friends one day, and dating came up. One of the ladies said, "When you sleep with a guy, it changes the relationship." We all agreed that was true. That's another reason it's so important to follow God's standards and principles. Sexuality is a powerful force that can draw you together, but outside God's approval, it can become a destructive force that eventually destroys intimacy and scars hearts. Making the decision to wait until marriage before sharing your body honors and pleases God. It sets an example for others and highlights the love you have for God. It is your special way of loving, serving, and honoring Him. It also protects your heart and emotions.

When you give your body to your husband, you're investing a deep part of you in the relationship. You become one with him physically and make a lasting soul connection. And the same is true when a husband gives his body to his wife. Sex is the highest human form of "knowing" someone. The Word of God says Adam "knew" Eve, and she conceived. When intimacy is in the order God designed, this "knowing" always bears fruit. For instance, when you "know" God in an intimate and personal way, you bear the fruit of the Spirit and bear or reveal the attributes of Christ to the world. The same happens when you "know" a man and a man "knows" you as a woman. Something is always birthed from the exchange, whether it be more love, commitment, fear, rejection, pain, or shame. Therefore, know for your own sake that keeping your body pure is not only a way of worshipping and honoring God, it is also a way of guarding your heart.

Every command of God was given to protect you and your

relationship with Him. When it comes to sexuality, He doesn't want to prevent you from experiencing pleasure. God doesn't want you to walk around with a shattered heart, low self-esteem, or a torn spirit. As you surrender willingly and joyfully to Him and follow His instructions, you'll find safety for your heart and the lasting peace and joy He gives when you are in the center of His will.

Dear Michelle,

I love God and everything, but this whole celibacy thing is a big problem. The minute I tell a guy I'm saving myself for marriage, he's gone. Even the single guys at church push for sex early in a relationship. They act like not having sex before marriage is unreasonable and unfair.

At this rate I doubt if I'll ever get married! If I can't get a man to consistently date me, how will I ever get to the altar? I have faith, but the reality is there are too many women willing to compromise sexually, so they seem to have an edge over me. And there doesn't seem to be enough men to go around, so competition is already fierce enough.

What's a girl to do? I've been waiting a long time, and to be totally honest, I'm tired of it. I'm beginning to doubt if there is someone out there for me. And I'm wondering how much my unwillingness to compromise sexually is costing me. I mean really, people sleep with each other every day and a lot of them do get married eventually. Is sex before marriage really that bad? I'm at a crossroad between what the church teaches about sex and what I've been longing for far too long in my opinion.

Why doesn't God just take the desire for intimacy away if He isn't going to bring a man into my life who wants to marry me? I'm not feeling so sassy, single, and satisfied these days. Tell me something that will help, please!

Yours truly,
Feeling Conflicted

Dear Conflicted,

I feel your pain. I'm going to keep it real with you. Let's face it, you and I have heard all there is to say on this matter, and it's beginning to sound trite. Sex is actually not a deal maker or deal breaker in a relationship. Whether you believe it or not, there are still good men who are surrendered to God and want to wait until after the "I do's" to make love. For now, the ball is in your court. You get to decide what kind of man you want. Do you want one who won't break God's heart or one who will cause you to wonder if he's exercising physical discipline when you aren't with him?

Your decision to walk in purity must be based totally on your love for God if you want to be successful. If you make love with a man in the expectation that it will bind him to you, you're setting yourself up for great heartache—with God and with the man. Girl, you do not need to be singing, "Will you still love me tomorrow?"! You do not need to set yourself up to struggle with the knowledge you sinned and the consequences of that, which occur even though God will forgive you.

You want to be confident that the man in your life loves you, desires you, sees you as a prize worth waiting for, and honors God's standards. And the right man will also help you stand strong in your decision to honor God's standards, just as you help him.

Like Solomon wrote, "My darling bride is like a private garden, a spring that no one else can have, a fountain of my own" (Song of Solomon 4:12 TLB). The woman Solomon speaks of was asked by her brothers whether she was like a door or a wall:

> If she is a wall [discreet and womanly], we will build upon her a turret [a dowry] of silver; but if she is a door [bold and flirtatious], we will enclose her with boards of cedar.

And the woman responded,

> [Well] I am a wall [with battlements], and my breasts are like the towers of it. Then was I in [the king's] eyes as one [to be respected and to be allowed] to find peace (Song of Solomon 8:9-10 AMP).

Each time you engage in sex outside of marriage, you're investing yourself not just physically but spiritually as well. You've become one with that person, creating a bond that can't be severed. You feel the pain of separation when you part. Your spirit and heart get torn. Your spirit can suffer deeply if you allow your heart to harden and turn away from listening to the Holy Spirit. Is it that deep? Yes, it is, friend. And there is no such thing as casual sex.

Physical contact isn't a promise, so it just makes sense to keep that which is precious in a safe place until someone loves, honors, and protects you enough to marry you and wait until after the vows are said to become one with you.

Some people treat their possessions with more respect and honor than their own bodies! In fact, there are even legal ramifications when you are intimate with someone without being married. All the people I know who lived together never married each other. And when some of the men in those relationships died, their children from previous relationships showed up, kicked the women out of the house, and took everything. The live-in women had no legal rights or recourse, so they had to deal with that on top of their grief. Don't let a man, the prevailing culture, or your biological clock pressure you into violating God's *standards that are in place to protect and help you. Remember, His principles stay the same regardless of how society's views change.*

How long must you fight temptation and stay pure? As long as it takes. God will bless your commitment to following His Word!

Here's to clarity!
Michelle

Keeping It Real

What you do with your heart and your body will always be determined by your estimation of your own value. Most items purchased in a store are bought on faith that they will work when the purchaser gets them home. It is true that at some places samples are given to encourage sales, but that is risky business. A sample might convince someone they don't like the product! By purchasing the item, they are saying, "Wow! Look what I found! I can't wait to take it home."

Now, of course, people who sleep together do often get married, but usually the man isn't in a rush because his desires are being fulfilled. As my mother says, "Why buy the cow when you can get the milk for free?" Ultimately the decision is up to you. How much do you love God and desire to follow Him—even when it's difficult? Yes, the enemy of your soul will do all he can to get you to compromise. And if you compromise, he'll kick into high gear and do all he can to make you feel condemned and unworthy of approaching God to ask for forgiveness. Living with regret is a terrible thing. When relationships that included sexual intimacy end, some pain is from the man leaving, yes, but I believe the majority of remorse is from the rejection of the precious parts of your heart, body, and spirit you shared through sex. You gave parts of yourself that you can never get back.

Yes, the Bible states that sin is pleasurable for a season, but remember that "the wages of sin is death" (Romans 6:23). We die slowly, by degrees, when we step out from under the protection of God. If you have sinned, remember that God loves you and cares about you. He's waiting for you to come to Him and ask for forgiveness! When you do, His grace will flow over you, cleansing your heart and spirit and restoring your relationship with Him. This leaves room for healing to come and the hope that you will love again. And this time you'll be much wiser.

17
Closing the Deal

For many navigating through the field of dating and relating, the experience is one thing but getting to the altar is another. How does one go from being a date to being a mate? What separates those who are still waiting from those who have closed the deal? Two words sum it up: being intentional. You need to be intentional. Every boat will continue to float aimlessly until it is steered toward a destination.

My mother often tells the story of dating my father. After a year of wonderfulness she said to him, "Well, it's been nice knowing you." His reply was one of wondering what she was talking about. She said, "I have enjoyed being with you, and I love you very much. But I can't continue to date you forever. I believe a man should know what he wants to do after a year, so I feel I must move on." To which my father replied that she wasn't going anywhere because they were getting married!

My mother was right. In most cases, a man knows what he wants to do. He gets that "Adam" vibe deep down in his spirit that names his woman. He recognizes her and names her. Now, since humans are no longer in the garden, men have meandered, and they drag their feet when it comes to making lasting covenants. As I've said, the normal man will not do anything he doesn't have to when it comes to the person he's dating. So if you're satisfied with a three-year courtship, he will be too. I don't know of many women who are pleased with that type of arrangement! They simply go along with it, not rocking the boat because they're afraid their men will bolt if they bring up the issue of marriage. No woman who truly values herself will go along with indefinite dating. The only exception, in my view, is if she and her man have a specific time line they've both agreed to.

Remember, perhaps the greatest aspect of walking in purity in your relationship, after the fact that it pleases God, is that it moves both people toward making a decision on where the relationship is going more quickly. The understanding is that to enjoy the full benefits of the relationship, you must be married.

If you've already messed that up, how do you get back on track? By keeping your eye on the prize and not settling for less than what you want from the relationship. Yes, this will require making difficult choices and instituting discipline on your part that will be difficult. If you eat snacks all the time, you will never enjoy the gourmet meal when you arrive at the destination. This is a discussion you will need to have with your man. Let him know how you feel when you disobey God. Tell him you don't want further disobedience to mar your romance. You want to keep your relationship positive and not let guilt undermine the relationship. You also don't want to be responsible for encouraging him to step outside God's will. Then discuss and set the boundaries you both need to keep the relationship and stay pure until you marry. This discussion will let him know how much you want to stay with him and emphasize that you're not rejecting him. It also lets him be part of the decision, solution, and follow-through efforts. This process won't be easy, but it starts with a decision and continues with a plan for success.

When you are intentional about getting to a specific place, all your choices, including navigating the twists and turns, are designed to get you to your destination. If you don't believe you'll get there, that's when compromise sneaks its way into your journey. That's when you find yourself taking long forays into things that take you well off your path.

Alfred, Lord Tennyson wrote in his poem *In Memoriam*, " 'Tis better to have loved and lost than never to have loved at all." I don't think I agree with that! The pain of separation after you've been in love and the person walks away can be devastating, leaving your heart shattered and your soul fractured. If you haven't had that experience, you are still whole! What am I saying? Not only should you not compromise, you need to be very clear where you want to go. If you don't stand for something, you will fall for anything.

So is your desired destination the marriage altar? Then you can't afford to take shortcuts. You can't stop and fill up on "junk food" experiences in your relationship. You know, those instant gratification-fillers that satisfy in the moment but have no nutritional value. These empty calories just add weight to the relationship that you don't want, making it unhealthy while killing the hunger for real food. What do these junk-food fillers look like? Giving way too much of yourself before marriage. Don't be a wife until you are a wife, I say. The man in your life needs to be consumed by thoughts of how to get more of you—more of your time, more of your help, more of who you are. If you give him too much too early, he has nothing to long for.

If your goal is marriage, focus on getting there and not turning down another street. If he starts to steer off the road, you need to do a GPS check—a "God Positioned Satellite" check for your position. Don't assume you're being taken where you want to go. Ask questions without demanding specific answers or whining. Just ask nicely, "Where are we in this relationship? Where are we headed? I'm in love with you and can't help thinking about a future with you. I'm wondering if you feel the same way too. Do you?"

In the movie *The Back-up Plan,* Zoe (played by Jennifer Lopez) had a great fear of rejection that caused her to overreact to the slightest thing her love interest said. She eventually totally pushed him away. He loved her deeply but could no longer deal with her outburts. Zoe's nana finally told her she would never have a lasting relationship if she kept pushing every man away. It was time to face her fear. This was also my malady, which a friend thankfully pointed out to me. As I reviewed my relationships, I saw the pattern. She was right.

In the interest of protecting myself, I realized that I guarded my heart right from the starting gate of the relationship. I shuddered at the thought of being so vulnerable that I would actually express need, pain, fear, or anything that might imply I needed a man's help and trusted him to handle my heart responsibly and with great care.

Now there is a thin line between being vulnerable and setting yourself up for rejection and heartbreak. While reviewing a relationship that had gone south, my wise spiritual mother said something that resonated in my heart. "You feel terrible about how this worked out because you were never honest with the guy. If you had shared how you really feel, we would not be having this discussion. You left the door open for him to do exactly what he is doing now. If you had been more forthcoming and he still chose to walk away, you would at least be empowered by knowing you had been your authentic self with him. Now all you're left with are scenarios of what would have happened if..."

Needless to say, that got my attention. I went to my man and told him exactly how I felt. He was shocked! And I thought I'd been totally obvious all along. Even though I was known for giving wise relationship advice, I'd forgotten that most men don't pick up on a woman's subtle innuendos and hints. They don't "see the signs" we think are apparent. They need us to be direct! So when you're with your man, spell it out, make it plain, and keep it real. This needs to become your mantra when dealing with the man you're interested in. Of course, you must do it sweetly and within healthy boundaries. Blowing him away with a full barrel blast of emotion isn't your goal. Getting to the marriage altar with the right man is.

The greatest key to closing the deal is you knowing how much your love is worth.

Like us, men need to know it's safe before they'll ask questions that might reveal their mindset and hearts. Therefore, help them feel safe enough with you that they won't fear rejection. Let them know you are intentional about the relationship and want them to be as well.

One of my shih tzu dogs, Matisse, loves to meander when I take him out to "do his business." When I get tired of waiting and head for the house, he knows it's his last chance, so he finally goes. If I kept patiently waiting, who knows how long he'd take! It takes my signal that his time is up for him to do what he has to do. The same thing holds true with men. And if you let a man know the parameters and he leaves, well, you've weeded out someone who wanted to keep you on a string so he could enjoy the benefits of a relationship without an end goal in mind.

My last piece of advice on closing the deal is that you must be willing to walk away. Love that isn't tested seldom endures. This is not a manipulation move on your part; it's just a logical response to the situation. If the relationship seems like it's in a stalemate, you need to make a decision in the interest of clearing the deck for someone who is ready to get to know you and, if he's the right one, willing to commit to you. At the end of the day, you know you are a woman worth knowing and keeping. If the guy in your life doesn't realize that yet, he doesn't deserve more of your time, heart, or emotions. The greatest key to closing the deal is you knowing how much your love is worth!

Dear Michelle,

I've been dating the same guy for six years. We have a great relationship and do everything together. Our families and friends are all intertwined. Yet every time I bring up the subject of marriage, he either avoids it like the plague or says he isn't ready. How can he not know what he wants to do after six years? Am I missing something here? I don't know what he's waiting for.

We are both financially sound, so that isn't an excuse. We both own homes and live comfortably. I keep thinking that if I don't make it that big of an issue he will eventually see the light, but I see time slipping away. I thought by now we'd have settled down and be having children. Instead I am still waiting to get to second base. How do I get him to move from indecision to a permanent commitment?

Truly Lost in Transition

Dear Lost,

What are you missing? You're missing courage at this point to do the only thing you need to do in this situation—kick that man to the curb or drop him like he's hot. Six years? Really? You've allowed someone to waste six years of your life? My dear sister, when a man says he doesn't know what he wants to do or he's not ready for marriage after that long, he is actually saying he isn't ready for marriage to you.

You will eventually break up with this man, and I predict he will be married to someone else in a matter of six months, if not less. When a man drags his feet this long, it is an indication of how he feels about you. If you continue to allow him to coast with you until he sees what he really wants, you're setting yourself up for serious heartbreak. The only way you can find out now how he really feels about you is to get out of the relationship. He will either decide he can't live without you and put a ring on your finger or he will let you go. And that, my friend, would be the best favor he could do for you.

Don't waste more time on this one. Your life is not a game, and he should not have a monopoly on your life. Do not pass go or collect $200. Simply say bye-bye. Six years! I don't know how you stayed pure that long...or is that another part of the problem?

'Nuff said!
Michelle

Keeping It Real

Friend, never give a man the luxury of wasting your time. Every day you spend with him is a day you're off the market. Some men will string you along because they are selfish. They don't want you permanently, but they like what you add to their lives. If they can feed you just enough carrots to keep you around, that works for them. Don't let them. You're simply putting off the hurt that's coming your way. It will arrive eventually, and you'll be more angry at yourself for allowing the relationship to drag on the way it did.

Keep your goal in mind. Set a time limit based on a reasonable dating period and how long you can afford to wait. Stick to your deadline, and be willing to walk. This is a gamble you must take because your future is at stake. You can't afford to allow someone to have that much power over your future if he is not willing to make a full investment. Think of it this way. He is standing in the way of what you truly desire—a lifetime of love with a partner who sees and recognizes your worth. And that is a prize great enough to put a relationship on the line for.

18

The Language of Love

At one point in history, people decided to get together and build a tower to the sky to see whatever they could see. The news of these events reached heaven, and God counseled with Himself (the Trinity) and decided to come down and see what the people were doing. His comment on their activities was interesting. He concluded that because they were one people and spoke one language, nothing would be impossible to them. Their unity would make them invincible! They would be able to accomplish anything their hearts desired. So He mixed up their languages to stop them from exalting themselves above Him (Genesis 11:1-11 MSG). And, girlfriend, even though this created the languages of nations, there's an interesting parallel that brings it home to you and your partner. Communication between the sexes can be just as mixed up and difficult!

When two people come together in marriage, they become one physically, yes, but they also start the marriage-long process of becoming a unified entity. And with Jesus Christ at the center of their marriage, the couple can stand as a powerful force against all the world can throw at them. God is putting the two of you together to form a powerful team for His glory and the furtherance of His kingdom. Like it says in Ecclesiastes 4:12, "A cord with three strands is not quickly broken." The team united in Christ and in each other wins. A powerful aspect of this unity is the special communication that develops between a husband and wife. When a look can telegraph an entire paragraph on what their positions are, their opponents fight an uphill battle. When one word tells an entire story between them, that creates a powerful wall of unity.

As a couple, you need to learn each other's languages so you can communicate quickly and effectively. This is especially helpful in times of conflict. My mentor P.B. Wilson told me she had to learn to speak "Franklish," a cute way of saying she learned to speak so her husband, Frank, could understand immediately. She learned his way of relating so he knew what she was saying quickly and clearly without misinterpretation.

To learn your man's language, you must be silent and observe. Listen to his cues. What does he reference when he's talking about things and describing events? Is he an audio person—preferring words—or a visual person—preferring diagrams and drawings? Does he describe things by sounds or does he paint word pictures? What are the things he's passionate about? Perhaps he is a sports buff, so a great way to communicate with him will be through that terminology. He will get what you're saying because you're giving him examples he can relate to.

Men like things spelled out. They don't like to guess at meanings. They aren't as naturally intuitive as women are, so having to guess what you mean can be frustrating for them. Your man wants you to tell the truth and make it plain. He wants you to know what you want so you can tell him what that is. In other words, don't present problems to him that don't have potential solutions. He wants to know what you want and is usually happy to follow through to help you be happy. What sidelines him is when you don't communicate clearly with him. If you don't know your needs, how can he? As a husband, he'll be given the charge to take care of you the same way he does his own body. And when it comes to his own body, he knows what he wants. When it comes to you, he needs to know what you want and have you communicate that in a gentle, easy way that equips him to help you. I encourage you to start discovering how to most effectively communicate early in your relationship.

So what if you're unhappy? How do you get your point across without making the situation even worse? First, take a personal inventory. Have you been the woman he needs and done all you can for him within the level of your current relationship? If you have a concern you want to bring up, will he have a list of his own to present to you? You're not thinking this through to avoid conversation but to be ready for openness on his side too.

Think carefully about what is bothering you, and what you would like him to do to make the situation better. Keep it realistic. Don't bring up an issue when anger is active. The goal is to be heard without the other person feeling the need to defend himself. And do not bring up issues via text, email, or other means of communication that often leave the door wide open to major misinterpretation of what is being shared. Talk face-to-face quietly, without accusation, presenting your needs and suggestions in a way that will allow him to be your hero. Be willing to partner with him to help him get it right. That means celebrating with him when he's right and resisting the urge to browbeat him when he isn't. Let the conversation be more about "we" and less about finger-pointing and blame. Let him know your needs, how you feel when your needs are overlooked, and what he can do to help the situation now and in the future.

Keep in mind that your reality is yours, and his reality is his. They are different. As a couple, each person's point of reference and view needs to be acknowledged, and often adjustments have to be made to gain understanding. Sometimes it may come down to agreeing to disagree. Not every conflict has to be resolved on the spot. Some may remain open to be resolved at a later date, perhaps giving both of you time to grow, consider the situation in more detail, or adjust to the idea of the changes needed. You want to both be in a place where you can own what you're hearing.

And speaking of "owning" stuff, you also must be willing to own where you're coming from in the relationship while being open to hearing his side of the story and how he perceives your actions. Most actions are responses to other actions. Don't let your conversation turn into trying to win a personal victory. Instead, find a place where you win together as a couple. Sometimes the victory of being right is short-lived if you find yourself right but alone. Every conflict should lead to resolution, not further chaos. So approach problems with an attitude geared toward reconciliation instead of proving a point. Focus on what you want your relationship to look like long term. Keep pride and assumption out of the picture and meet with open hearts to hear and be heard.

Dear Michelle,

I am at a complete loss as to how to get through to my man. I've given up on trying to talk to him, so now I just don't say anything. Of course, that drives him crazy. Then he starts following me around and asking me what's wrong. When I say nothing, he continues to press the issue until I explode.

Once I get started, it's hard for me to stop. I go on and on, and he gets this glazed-over look in his eyes that lets me know that even though he's pretending to listen he really isn't. It's so frustrating because nothing changes. Why can't I get through to him? Should I just throw in the towel and move on? How do I get my point across and have the light go on instead of off in his eyes?

I feel as if we're living in two different worlds. I can't name the planets, but they are not in sync at all!

Sincerely,
Fresh Out of Words

~~~

Dear Fresh Out,

That is probably the best place you could be right now. The glazed look in his eyes is a signal that you've overplayed your hand. You didn't state what your exact issue was. Hopefully it was something much deeper than him not calling you as many times as you'd like or how he leaves the toilet seat when he visits you. Whatever it is, you need to reverse your strategy. Stop torturing the man. Stop being a silent victim.

The silent treatment is not a good look on any woman. It can mar the most beautiful countenance. Woman up! Sit down with your man, take his hands in yours, and stroke them. Be sweet, pleasant, and nonthreatening. Kill the attitude of silent suffering because it never accomplishes anything. Tell him you love him and you love being with him. You want to open up the communication lines so you both can enjoy your relationship even more.

Ask him how he's feeling and if there is anything he needs from you. When he responds, listen carefully and let him know you're interested and what you'll do.

When he asks if you need anything from him, share how you've been feeling and what specifically has been bothering you. He might well be surprised you've been feeling that way. He'll ask what he can do to help you feel better about the situation. This is when you can help him help you. Tell him what you need. Be specific while being open to discussing if it's workable or what modifications can be made. Don't force him to make promises he can't keep, and don't expect him to get it right that second. Be open to working with your man. Make sure he knows you appreciate his efforts to address your needs.

Most men aren't confrontational naturally. They run from discussions and controversies that are personal in nature, so
~~~

you have to help him feel safe before you can have a fruitful exchange. Once he feels that you're not the enemy and that you will love him no matter what, he will relax and receive what you have to say. And don't forget what I said about using language he can understand. Speaking "his" language will save a lot of time and aggravation, giving you more time for positive interactions.

Here's to letting him know
what you really need.
Michelle

Keeping It Real

First, let me bring up instant communication. Today it's so easy to misinterpret messages sent via technology. Texting, pinging, and emailing should be reserved for short updates. Deep conversations should be face-to-face. Most messages leave much open to the imagination. Without facial expressions and other cues, it's too easy to miss someone's intent or attitude. That's one reason I don't recommend this type of communication for conflicts or life-changing conversations. Two more reasons to avoid technological communication are that it's too easy to say way more than you should and what you say can be brought up again and again because it's out there to be interpreted any which way. Please consider your communication methods and words carefully. It may be kept and referred back to time and time again. Always double-check to make sure you're sending the message to the right person before hitting the send button.

So what's the best way to communicate when you have something important to share? The Bible says an offended brother is more unyielding than a fortified city (Proverbs 18:19). You will not get through to a man who feels he has to defend himself against you. Neither will you get through to a man who doesn't feel listened to or respected. It is critical for the health of your relationship that your man knows his heart, his thoughts, and his emotions are safe with you. He may be open to listening to your needs, but he will shut down in the face of demands.

Also remember you are not his mother. Deal with him as a man. Stay in control of your emotions, engaging your mind even while feeling with your heart. Your power as a woman to influence him and inspire him to rise to the occasion to meet your needs is one of the greatest natural gifts you possess. My mother says there is a reason God gave us two ears and one mouth—so that we will listen more than we speak. Communication goes two ways, so make sure to listen and acknowledge what your man says. Understanding breeds understanding. Set a positive atmosphere, create a receptive mood for listening to one another's hearts, and then share tenderly and honestly. Give your man the room he needs, and watch him fulfill your expectations.

19

Then Comes Marriage

It's been said that marriage is like a fortified city. Those who are outside want to get in and those who are inside want to get out. This is a foreign concept for singles who have been hoping and wishing and praying for mates for a long time. They can't conceive of reasons why a married person would want to be single again. And yet many singles also wonder if there are any happy marriages because they hear so many complaints coming from the other side of the fence. It can be rather disturbing. Even more alarming are the high numbers of newlyweds who declare they didn't sign up for what was occurring in their marriages. When they talk to me, I always ask what they thought they were signing up for!

Marriage fantasies die quickly after both parties say "I do" and the real work of marriage begins. Television, movies, and other media make it look so easy. They never show people's mundane routines. They seldom show them struggling to pay the bills, going to work, or coming home exhausted. They seldom show the communication struggles, the worrying that happens in the middle of the night, or the problems in sexual relations. No, media tends to glorify everything, even though one spouse is usually clueless (to make the sitcoms work). And when there are problems in these shows, they are quickly resolved without too much effort. After one or two dramatic turns, things just magically work out. People fall back in love and ride off into the sunset in a blaze of passion. Sad to say, this is not the case in real life.

Although marriage can be wonderful, it also has its mundane moments. People have bad breath in the morning. They don't feel passionate all the time. People have annoying habits they've had for a long time and will have trouble breaking if they ever try to. Individuals who have been alone a long time have issues with sharing...their space, their time, their anything. All of this can be disconcerting as well as disappointing if you're not prepared for the reality of two people coming together to *become* one day in and day out. The key word there is "become." The union of your spirits and lives doesn't meld together overnight. It happens over time as God works in both of you, and you both grow spiritually, which includes dying a little every day. With God's help, you put to death selfishness, pride, insistence on your own way, preconceived notions of what your life should look like...and, shucks, even what your man would be like as your husband.

Marriage demands the dismantling of yourself completely in order to rebuild two people into one strong unit. So if you have any ideas that marriage is going to make you happy and be the period on the sentence that is your life, think again. It is the graduate level of study for your life, and if you want to master it you have to throw out all notions of what you expect and what you will get out of it. It is only when you change your mindset to what you can give to the other person that you will begin to grow and be joyfully fulfilled in the relationship.

This goes back to understanding the meaning of love as a decision to give of yourself—not 50 percent, but 100 percent. It is when you get to the place of exercising patience, kindness, and all the other fruit of the Spirit while allowing your spouse his humanity—flaws and all—that you begin to walk out this thing called marriage and reap satisfying fruit. When you see happily married couples, they have weathered some things together. They have died to self and decided to live in one another, much as we do when we come to Christ and say "no longer I but Christ in me." Marriage is the physical manifestation of our spiritual relationship with Christ. In Christ we die to ourselves so that His attributes will come alive in us and dominate our character. He renews our minds to be in agreement with His point of view, which then transforms our lives as we grow in Him and our character, attitudes, and choices change. We become more like Jesus, which makes us infinitely better and greater. More fruitful. More victorious. More joyful. More fulfilled.

In marriage, to grow and become one we must let go of ourselves and our insistence on the way things should be done and the way life should happen. Instead, we become open to the possibilities of what life can look like as we embrace the people in our lives and say yes to becoming one with them. Then we balance the best parts of one another, accept one another's weaknesses and flaws, and resist the urge to fix our mates because we are trusting God to build up those areas.

On the practical side, we've all experienced the rush of new love. Research is revealing that part of that reaction is caused by the hormone oxytocin, which is released when we experience positive emotions, touch, and interactions. But hormone levels go up and down, and stress can deplete oxytocin. Time also depletes this hormone, but it can be renewed. After the initial spark of love, the level usually dies down after a year or so. Then it must be rekindled with interactions that remember and renew your "first love" experiences. Why am I bringing this up? Because love and relationships require work. In order for your marriage to be the relationship you had in mind, you'll need to do some things to maintain or increase the romance, communication, understanding, and unity both of you will need to go the distance.

Love is a verb as well as a noun, so be willing to take action. Make the decision to invest in the things that will help keep your relationship vibrant. As the saying goes, "You've got to do what you did to catch them in order to keep them." Or, as God might put it, you have to keep returning to your first love. Saying "I do," is just the beginning. The maintenance and growth of a relationship requires effort. If you don't do the work, the relationship will fail. God told the church in Ephesus that they needed to remember how their relationship with Him began. He asks them to repent and go back to what they'd experienced at first (Revelation 2:4). Your marriage relationship requires similar action. It's so easy to overlook those days and months of first love when you're going through the day-to-day routines of married life. Sometimes it's hard to give of yourself completely and keep consistent in your attention to love and service because the pressures of life and survival can distract and deplete your energy and coping skills.

I encourage you to be sensitive to when passion wanes so you can do what you need to stir it back up. I have an idiosyncrasy that might be more appropriate than I originally thought. When referring to a wedding, I often mistakenly use the word "funeral." In an odd way, there are parallels. By falling in love and choosing to marry, you've signed up for a lifetime of dying to self, of becoming less of you every day so you can become more "one" with your spouse. This can be an amazing experience if you're willing to keep growing as an individual and as a couple. "As iron sharpens iron, so a friend sharpens a friend" (Proverbs 27:17 NLT). And so do spouses to an even greater degree! If you view marriage as an opportunity for refinement and growth, the cherry on top of the cake will be the continued romance and passion that will come from growing together. And that makes marriage worth signing up for.

Dear Michelle,

I have a wonderful man in my life. He wants to get married, but I have to admit I'm not attracted to him. I love everything else about him. He is strong spiritually, very attentive, kind, and he really loves me. He honors me and takes very good care of me. He's a hard worker and a nice person, but the fireworks and passion just aren't there for me. I know he would be a really good husband. What should I do? He's been waiting several months now for my *answer. I'm so afraid of blowing a good thing that I don't know what to do.*

Am I expecting a fantasy when it comes to romance? I don't want to make a decision I'll regret. Please advise; I'm truly in a quandary.

What Would You Do?

Dear WWYD,

If I were you, I'd pray and wait until I received God's peace about a decision. Now that I've said that, let me share a few schools of thought with you.

Many years ago my pastor's wife, who knew I was prone to over-spiritualizing everything at that stage in my life, gave me some very sound advice. She said, "Michelle, when you get married, make sure you like the person, love the person, and are 'in love' with the person." What does this mean? You are a woman with a spirit and soul that dwells in a physical body. In marriage, you want all dimensions of you to be satisfied. Although ultimately the purpose of marriage is to work out God's design in two people that He brings together for a greater purpose than personal pleasure, your partner should appeal to you. Why shortchange someone by marrying him without desiring him?

You mentioned a lot of great things about this man, but you didn't really give details on why you don't desire him. Is he unattractive? Not your type? What? Usually with that many good things going on, a person would naturally fall in love with him. During that process, he would become more attractive to you even if he wasn't what you initially had in mind. I suggest you search your heart for any preconceived notions, unrealistic expectations, or fears that might be keeping you from *completely loving this man you have been blessed to have in your life.*

If after your heart search you still have no peace about saying yes, then do the right thing and release him so he can find someone who will love and treasure him as he deserves. That is only fair. By doing this, you also release yourself to be free to be found by a person you will be attracted to in every way.

Don't waste any more of his time or your own. Don't keep him around because he's a good friend or it's convenient. You will only be blocking blessings for him and you. Say yes or let him go.

Trusting God to give you peace,
Michelle

Keeping It Real

When deciding whether to marry, you should remind yourself that divorce will never be an option. Ask your guy if he feels the same way. Commit to each other that divorce will never be brought up, especially during a disagreement.

Next, ask these important questions:

- Can I live with this person for the rest of my life if he never changes?
- Does this person add to my sense of purpose and destiny?
- Does he add to my life?
- Do I add to his?

The Word of God says, "Two are better than one, because they have a good return for their labor" (Ecclesiastes 4:9) and "He who finds a wife finds what is good and receives favor from the LORD" (Proverbs 18:22). The "favor" comes from being in right relationship with God and with your spouse. These right relationships spur you on to good works that will bear rich fruit in your life and fill you with peace, joy, and fulfillment. Who could ask for anything more than that?

20

Cheating, Lying, and Other Love Traps

Out of the seven things God hates, lying is on the list. I am with Him. Nothing sets me off worse than the knowledge that someone has lied to me. Now, please understand a lie can take two forms: 1) a blatant untruth and 2) something is not said that leads someone to believe something that isn't true. Both are deliberate attempts at deception and can be major deal breakers in any relationship. We may not always like the truth, but it will set us free. God likes truth. He says even though we're deeply stained by sin we should come to Him, expose our error by admitting the truth, and ask for His forgiveness. He says He will grant it! The same basically holds true in our human relationships too, except we reason together until we come to a place of reconciliation. It's the deep, dark, undercover stuff that wrecks relationships. Sweeping things under the rug and operating as if everything is fine causes an even bigger mess when the deception is discovered.

Truth is of paramount importance in any relationship. Don't overlook lies, and don't make or allow excuses for the liar. Lies put cracks in the foundation of a relationship, and some are almost impossible to repair. Many people aren't willing to do the work it takes to recover a relationship after deception or unfaithfulness. Proverbs 20:6 asks,

"Many claim to have unfailing love, but a faithful person who can find?" If God asked the question through His Word, that lets us know deception is very real.

Faithful men do exist! Let's focus on two types of men right now. One type has what I call a "conventional" spirit. He would rather play it safe than be sorry. He wants to chart his course slow and steady with no surprises or drama. He wants a relationship he can count on, a woman he can trust, and the certainty that his romantic relationship is settled so he can focus on the business of living and achieving, period... or, as the British say, full stop. Then there is the type of man who has an "unfaithful" spirit. This man is wired to wander. It has nothing to do with the woman in his life or what she is or isn't doing. His woman shouldn't take his wandering personally. It's his issue, not hers. Can he be rehabilitated? Yes, but only by the Holy Spirit. Weeping, accusing, confronting—nothing a woman can do will stop this man from being who he is. He has to allow God to overhaul his spirit and heal his inner man to wholeness so he can be faithful.

The reason I explained these two types of men is so you can consider your part in their lives. The conventional man can become an unfaithful man, but he will have to be pushed over the line. Like Sarah handing her man Abraham over to Hagar to get a child, many women give their men away (Genesis 16). I'm sure I just heard somebody scream, "What?" Yes, it's true. What you won't do for love, someone else will. So, girl, you have to woman up and be on your job with your man. The secret to this is simple: Give him what he wants, not what you think he needs.

For example, say your man asks you for an apple. You decide he doesn't need the apple, so you give him an orange instead. Well, guess what? Though the orange may taste good and distract him from his hunger for a moment, eventually his initial desire will resurface and remind him that it is still unfulfilled. After all, he asked for an apple because that's what he really wanted. And along comes Sally, who gives him an apple. Now you're upset because Sally has his attention. I hope you're getting this principle. In a relationship, unless your man is asking you for something that violates the Word of God or is detrimental to you in some way, you need to address his needs and requests. This works both ways, of course, but we're talking about you right now. Remember that giving and serving are foundational elements in any successful exchange between two people.

The conventional man will become unfaithful only after a severe drought of his needs not being met. He can be pushed over the brink by a lack of respect, affection, attention, attraction/intimacy, or communication. He can be pushed over the brink by harshness, criticism, coldness, false accusations, nagging, pressure, and stress. I'm sure you get the idea. Here is where you have to do some deep soul searching. Ask yourself if you missed the hints your man was dropping when things started to go awry. Did you meet his needs? Did you listen to and follow bad advice from friends that has led to the demise of your relationship? Did your pride or selfishness become a factor? Did you stop taking care of yourself and looking your best? Did you stop doing what it took to get him in the first place? In today's world, women are on the prowl for good men. If they see one in need, many will do whatever they can to get his attention. So again, girl, be on your *job*!

The man with an unfaithful spirit is a whole different issue. In the name of finally being happy to have found someone, did you ignore all the warning signs that this man was a wanderer? Did you say to yourself that if you can just get the man to commit, everything else will work out? Not! "If it waddles like a duck and quacks like a duck, it's probably a duck!" So it stands to reason, if this man talks and walks like a player then he is a player! Women often walk a fine line because they love men who know what to do with a woman. The safer man, who is a little more low-key and has less swag, we find boring. Remember, the men who know what to do with a woman usually have had a lot of practice. This can be good or bad; it's just something to be aware of. If he's had a lot of practice and is now ready to use all that he's learned on one woman in a committed relationship, that's one thing. But if he is still practicing and seeing you at the same time, that's obviously bad.

Don't ignore the signs of problems. Don't convince yourself that he will change after you're married. He will not. Consider him an "as is" purchase. You know, just like at the store when that tag on a garment signifies you're agreeing to purchase it with the flaws. So if you are catching him in lies, cheating, or any of the things you don't like, you need to cut your losses, thank God for the information, and kick him to the curb! This is why the Bible says to guard your heart with all diligence (Proverbs 4:23). I adjure you not to be a silly woman who is led away by her desires and lusts. Don't settle for "something" because it won't necessarily be better than nothing if it will hurt you in the long run.

You need to count the costs of your relationship, be honest about what you want, and know what you are able and willing to live with. The thing you think you can't live without may be the thing that will eventually harm or kill you, so be careful and, if needed, cut your losses before they become greater. Remember Rachel, who told her husband Jacob, "Give me children or I'll die"? She got her wish, but eventually she died giving birth to her second son (Genesis 30:1; 35:16-18). When the Israelites forgot God's great blessings and went against what he said, God still gave them the desires of their hearts—even though it brought leanness to their souls (Psalm 106:13-15 AMP). Sometimes we insist on things God is trying to spare us from. Do your homework, my sistah. Take your time and assess your man and relationship honestly before making a commitment. And when you do commit and say "I do," you've made your choice and will be in covenant with your man before God. At that point you will have to follow the charge of fashion designer Tim Gunn: "You will have to make it work!"

Dear Michelle

I just found out the man I've been in love with for a year now has been seeing another woman the whole time he was seeing me! Michelle, I love this man. I am so shocked. He is kind, loving, sensitive...He says he doesn't know what happened, but he knows he wants to spend his life with me. He has ended it with the other woman and wants to focus on us.

What do I say? What do I do? I'm devastated that he deceived me all this time. He says he hadn't confirmed our *relationship, that he had told me we should just allow the relationship to grow and that I ran ahead of him.*

He is still very close to the other woman—as a matter of fact, they are starting a business together! I'm not sure their relationship is really over. He seems to be obsessed with her. He'll drop whatever he's doing and go to her if she calls. I feel that if it's really over, he would introduce me to her. He refuses to do that. Am I wrong to think I'm fighting a losing battle for his heart?

Tell Me If I'm Wrong

Dear Tell Me,

Whew! You've said a mouthful, and I think you know the handwriting is on the wall. If he was able to have a relationship with her all that time, something is up. He seems obsessed with her? Something is up. He won't introduce you to her? Something is definitely up! And now they're going into business together? Girlfriend!

Let me give you your options. You can either continue with this relationship and have no peace at all because you won't be able to trust him. Or you can cut your losses and move on. Oh sure, he didn't outright lie, but he didn't tell the truth either until it was convenient for him. That "let's just coast along and not define the relationship" line is old and used to leave a man's options open.

So he played his cards close to his chest until whatever happened between him and the other women caused him to try to make it work with you. Notice my words: Try to make it work. It doesn't sound like his heart is really in your relationship, given what he isn't willing to let go of. He and the other woman will be bound together through work, which will keep them *in constant contact. That will not be comfortable for you, and you'll always wonder if you can trust him.*

Girl, you should let go of him and keep stepping. Take care of your heart because he won't. If you choose to stick with him, you need to insist on meeting this woman, and he will have to agree to total disclosure and accountability to rebuild your trust. He should also give you a clear map for where the relationship is going. If he's not willing to do that, dump him! If the other woman is more important, there is a reason why—and you aren't part of it. I don't know any way to dress this one up, sistah.

I wish I could tell you
something different,
Michelle

Keeping It Real

Can the broken bridge created by unfaithfulness be mended? Absolutely! But it takes two people committed to complete transparency and accountability. That means your man does whatever you need him to do to rebuild your trust. If that is checking in to let you know where he is and what he's doing, so be it. Today's wonderful technology can be quite damaging to relationships as people text and ping away. These devices can be more dangerous and deeper than physical affairs in some ways. Because women are moved by what they hear and read, their worries are being heightened by technology as they fearfully check not only phone logs but text and ping histories. This reminds me of the song that says if you are looking for trouble you've come to the right place. Yes, I believe if you look for trouble, you'll find it. I suggest you don't do that. If you feel you need to, your relationship is already in trouble.

If you are a praying woman, you can ask God, and He will disclose what you need to know. He'll never leave you in the dark about what your man is doing. I'm a witness to that. Oh, I could tell you such stories! Through prayer, all things can be exposed. Through prayer your relationship can be restored if you and your man take the right steps to work through the issues that caused the problems to occur in the first place.

As I said before, don't take your man's unfaithfulness personally unless you've failed to meet his needs. If you know you've been on your job, you don't internalize the blame for his actions. If he wants to reconcile, get to the root of what was missing for him. Only if he is willing to be totally open to doing the work of rebuilding trust can the relationship be restored. Don't make it hard for him to do the work, but don't make it easy either. He can only get away with as much as you let him. Trust must be earned.

21

The Unacceptable Dilemma

Let's discuss the "A" word. Yes, I'm talking "A" as in "abuse." It's talked around more than it's talked about. It's painful, embarrassing, crushing to the spirit, destructive to the mind and self-esteem, and deadly. The bottom line is, "No abuse allowed!" This is a nonnegotiable in any relationship! Totally unacceptable.

There are several forms of abuse: The first that comes to mind and is the most obvious is physical, followed by mental and emotional abuse.

Physical Abuse

Let's look at physical abuse first. There is no reason for a man to put his hands on you except to help you through a door, up or down stairs, or to show you love and affection. Any other forms of contact, including slapping, punching, kicking, and throwing, should never be acceptable. If it occurs, never internalize it as being your fault. I don't care how much stress your man is under, what deep problems he has, what he's been through in the past, he should never consider hitting or hurting you in any way an option. God's design in man/woman relationships is for the man to protect and cover the woman, keeping her safe from harm or lack. It is a serious offense to mishandle a woman in the eyes of God.

My personal policy, which I hope is yours too, has always been if a man even threatens to hit me, it is the last chance he will get. If your man hits you once, he will hit you again. The violence and tendency to resort to it is in him. Don't make excuses. Don't blame yourself for the eruption of his temper. See him as he is—a man with a serious anger management problem you don't want to be subjected to.

When dealing with a man who will physically abuse you, part of the abuse will be mental. He will try to make you believe it is your fault. You pushed him over the edge. You pushed his buttons. You didn't know when to stop. You didn't follow his instructions. Couldn't you see he was tired? Stressed? Not one of these things is justifiable for a man putting his hands on a woman for harm. She is the physically weaker vessel to be protected and cherished. Whether a man is sick, drunk, stressed, or crazy—there is never a good reason for being violent toward someone he is supposed to love. And no woman should allow herself to believe it is her fault her man went ballistic.

There should also be immediate consequences for his actions. Until he is ready to get help for his lack of control, you need to remove yourself from being with him. If children are involved, all the more reason to separate your life from his. The effect abuse has on children is devastating. Consider their future if you won't consider your own. Your children may end up imitating his behavior or being attracted to abusers because that is what they grew up with. It's their normal.

As stress levels increase in life, I find it sad that women abusing men is on the rise. Whoever is doing the abusing needs to get counseling and deal with the root causes for this rage that does so much damage. The abused needs to find the courage to say this mode of behavior is unacceptable. Stop being a victim and fight for your love by getting on the path to wholeness. This will require strength on your part, which is why you can't allow him to play mind games with you or the children.

To be distracted by self-blame will deter you from getting the help you need. If you are busy thinking it is your fault or you make excuses or cover up the abuse, you will be distracted away from the main issue, which is your man's lack of self-control.

Getting to the root cause of what is brewing beneath the explosions is key to successfully healing his spirit and your relationship. This is work this man needs to do on his own. This will only occur if he feels he needs to do it. That usually won't occur unless he feels the sting of your absence and your unwillingness to facilitate or validate his dysfunction.

If you're just dating, that is a blessing. You need to leave the relationship. Don't minimize or ignore the abuse. Courtship is the time when people are on their best behavior, so if this occurs during that time, consider how much worse it will get. Get out of the relationship. Again I say do not pass go; do not collect $200. This man does not deserve to have a monopoly on your life (pun intended.) As a matter of fact, this man doesn't deserve to be in your life. He isn't healthy or ready to be with you. Many years ago, a guy I was dating rolled up a magazine and hit me with it. I can still remember the sting of it. I really loved this guy, but I have to tell you I made the decision to walk away. I refused to give him the opportunity to do that again.

Emotional and Mental Abuse

Emotional and mental abuse can be even more insidious than physical abuse. (For this discussion, I'm going to combine emotional and mental abuse under "emotional abuse.") Although physical abuse can leave scars, the deep scars on the psyche from emotional abuse can go deeper and completely shatter your sense of self and dissolve any shred of confidence you have left.

One tactic of a man who emotionally abuses is to systematically try to make you believe you're crazy. That everything you perceive is a figment of your imagination. He's critical, condescending, and cruel. He tries to make you question yourself—your desirability, your lovability, your worth, and even your intelligence. He wants to convince you that no one else can love you or even put up with you but him. That means, according to him, he is your best and only bet even though your association with him is painful at best.

Emotional abuse cuts to the core of who you are, and can be more painful and damaging than physical abuse. The attitude he presents to you. The silent treatment. The coldness. The looks of disdain. The caustic words. The put-downs in front of others. The way he belittles you in front of others. The berating for simple things. I know I may be pushing a lot of buttons here by weighing in on this so hard, but an abusive man is violating God's principles and love for you. God says a husband must care for his wife properly for his prayers to be heard (1 Peter 3:7). That is serious. God holds woman in such high esteem that He will not bless a man who abuses what He considers precious.

God doesn't create wounds; He binds them up. He doesn't rob you of your peace; He keeps you surrounded by it. He will not leave you comfortless. He will never insult His creation by calling you less than precious. He says you are fearfully and wonderfully made (Psalm 139)! He loves you so tenderly and carefully that He knows the number of hairs on your head. He paid a high ransom for you because He believes you're worth it. If the King of kings and Lord of lords thinks you're worth it, you'd better agree with Him! You are worth special treatment and care that leaves you feeling and looking your best as a wonderful representation of what God's woman looks like.

God created woman to be the glory of the man (1 Corinthians 11:7). How can woman be the glory of man if she isn't glowing with a sense of well-being and looking well loved and cared for? The greatest testimony besides what God has done in a husband's life is how his wife and household look. It speaks to who he is as a follower of Jesus and as a man. It speaks to the soundness of his character as he exemplifies and exhibits what God's care of His people looks like.

Any form of abuse is not within God's economy of love. It takes away from what He desires to build in every relationship—love, trust, and reliance. Don't allow *any* abuse in *any* of your relationships. Don't make room for it. Don't negotiate if it occurs. Don't rationalize it. Don't minimize it. Not one iota. An abuser doesn't see your value and doesn't esteem you as God desires.

Dear Michelle,

I don't know where else to turn at this point. I've been with my husband for three years. From the day we got married he changed. Every little thing sets him off, and he takes it out on me. I lost our first child because of it. He is so contrite afterward that I rethink if I should leave him. He cries and says he'll never do it again, but he does. It's so painful. I love him so much, but part of me feels it would be better to leave.

I spoke to my pastor about it, and he said I should pray and wait for God to change things. No one at church will confront him. Sometimes I think they believe it's my fault. I feel so defenseless. If I leave him they will say I am in sin and can't remarry. They will question my walk with the Lord. But what about my well-being? I'm afraid to leave and afraid to stay.

I don't know what to do. I feel guilty for being relieved that I lost my child rather than bring it into the center of a mess like this. Am I really in sin if I leave him? Please give me a real answer and not some canned Christian answer. At this point it is a matter of life and death. I have nothing left to lose.

Sincerely,
Broken

Dear Broken,

I find it very sad that you believe a real answer and a Christian answer aren't one and the same. Let me say this. Your husband is in sin for hitting you. You are the victim of his sin.

When we consider the heart of God, we can't divorce the fact that He always seeks the greater good above all things. There is no way that God would say you should stay in that situation. Any pastor who doesn't tell you to be safe first is violating God's principles and his own pastoral responsibility to you as a member of the church.

God does not approve or condone abuse and will not uphold it.

Should you immediately jump to divorce? Not necessarily. It depends on a lot of factors, including the type and severity of abuse, if your spouse accepts responsibility and truly repents, if he is open to counsel and correction, your own safety, and how you feel in your spirit about moving forward with him. Definitely get out of danger at once. I suggest a separation so he knows you're serious and feels the consequences of his actions. The reality that he could lose you might get through to him.

Both of you need to seek counsel. If the church you're attending condones or ignores the abuse, that is not a good place to seek help or accept advice. Seek a neutral, professional couselor. If your husband is not willing to take the steps necessary to get help, then sever ties with him. Find a healthier church environment that is not so legalistic that they wave away such a serious offense.

God does not want you in harm's way. Period. So, my dear, know this: God loves you. He wants you to be in a healthy, loving relationship. Take courage and leave. Let go...and leave that man to God. Go to where you are safe and have good and godly support.

I'm praying for you.
Michelle

Keeping It Real

The ramifications on the tribe of Benjamin were severe after some wicked men of the city of Gibeah in Benjamin raped and assaulted the wife of a traveler. Their abuse was so severe the woman died (Judges 19–21). When the husband of the concubine found his wife's body, he cut it up and sent pieces to every tribe of Israel so they would know of the atrocity. All the tribes of Israel except Benjamin gathered and went after the men who had violated the concubine. When the tribe of Benjamin refused to hand them over for justice, the other tribes declared war and destroyed all the towns of Benjamin and everything living within them. Thousands upon thousands of lives were lost. The avenging tribes of Israel swore they wouldn't allow their daughters to marry Benjamites. They were so serious about this declaration that they said anyone who did would be cursed. God gave the tribes victory to the point the Benjamite tribe was threatened with extinction! This story is deep, and other parts of it raise serious questions and concerns about the general attitude toward women held at that time. But it does show that abuse is not to be tolerated. There is a caveat regarding the hard-to-comprehend attitudes portrayed: "In those days there was no king in Israel; everyone did what was right in his own eyes" (Judges 21:25). Isn't that like today? But God is on His throne. He sees everything and holds people accountable for their actions.

Abusing a woman is serious to God! The result is costly to anyone who is involved. Make no mistake about it. No one should recommend or support a woman staying in danger by remaining with an abusive spouse.

If you're being abused and trying to decide your next move, let me say this: You only have one course of action: Take courage, grab hold of God's hand, and get safe. Allow God to be your protector as you position yourself out of harm's way.

If you know of someone in an abusive situation, don't allow her to suffer in silence and shame. Be supportive. Encourage her to get out and get help. It is a matter of life and death.

22

The Big "D"

Recently I heard that short-term marriage contracts were being explored. You know, where people would agree to be married for a specific time period, and at the end they would renegotiate or end the union amicably. The belief is this would solve a lot of issues, including avoiding costly divorces and eliminating some disappointment since both people had mutually agreed to remain married for a limited duration. I'm amazed at how people try to anticipate and divert pain. Given the bad reputation marriage has today, it's almost understandable why some people want to find a new alternative to offset what they fear.

Unfortunately, people are flawed and often don't keep their promises to one another, so quite a few marriages end in divorce today. For those who understand the depth of commitment implied in "covenant," which is what marriage is, it is no easy task to end a relationship and go their separate ways. But for far too many the towel gets thrown in before any real effort is made to reconcile their differences. Yes, the big "D" we're going to talk about is "divorce."

Someone asked me the other day "Why is it so easy for people to divorce these days?" I have several observations on this. Too many people marry for the wrong reasons. Many are driven by the sparks or chemistry, and that feeling dissipates in approximately a year, hopefully replaced by a deep and abiding love and appreciation for one another. People marry on the grounds of everything except what they should. After marriage, when the rose-colored glasses are no longer clear and initial passion wanes, they aren't prepared or equipped to do the work it takes to make a relationship work long term. Also, many couples don't have enough glue in their relationship to keep them together. The glue in this case consists of "commonalities and viewpoints"—shared visions and passions, gifts that are balanced between them, an appreciation of their differences, and, most of all, both people being *committed* to their commitment. Notice I said *both* people. A marriage can't be healthy if just one person stays committed. "Two becoming one" implies a *merging* of two wills, two minds, and two spirits agreeing on a single vision and purpose that causes them to walk together with a spirit of agreement. When these factors aren't present, the relationship will struggle, sometimes to the point of dissolution. As dissatisfaction grows, accusations fly and one or both will search for happiness and fulfillment elsewhere. The result is they drift further and further away from one another, with both parties eventually forgetting why they came together in the first place.

Another major factor is economics. Back in the day, people couldn't afford to walk away from their marriages. They had built their lives together and pooled their resources. Lots of women were stay-at-home wives and mothers without bank accounts of their own. People stayed together and made their relationship work because there were no other options. Now women are doing life for themselves, working outside the home for pay, sometimes achieving fabulous careers, and maintaining their own bank accounts and credit lines. That means they can afford to walk away from their marriages more readily. The more financially independent a person is, the more apt he or she is to say, "I don't have to stay here and deal with this." The tolerance for anything that feels even the slightest bit uncomfortable has dropped drastically, so the divorce rate has reached epidemic proportions in the world and in the church.

Why am I bringing divorce up when I know you aren't married? Because a huge population of single people fall into the divorced category. You are either single because you've never married, you are divorced, or you are widowed. Each category has its own issues. Divorce in many ways has been the scarlet letter in the church world with a disapproval ranking right up there with those who struggle with their sexual orientation. Many women, especially, have been made to feel like outcasts when their marriages didn't work out. They've been blamed, made to feel as if they are damaged goods, and that their lives can't be salvaged.

Many men and women have been made to feel guilty about wanting to marry again. They've been told the consequences of divorce include having to remain single for the rest of their lives to avoid committing adultery. Oh the pain I see in women's eyes when they ask me if it's true they can never hope for another love relationship. This interpretation hangs off the theology of one Scripture verse that has been sorely misinterpreted as "If someone who is divorced remarries he or she is guilty of adultery." What this verse is really saying is that if a husband divorces his wife to marry another, *he* commits adultery unless his wife was sexually unfaithful to him. (Remember, we're focusing on the man in this discussion.) Various theologians have searched Scripture and found that permissible grounds for divorce is adultery, but also abuse and abandonment. Is divorce permissible by God? Though He hates divorce, it is permissible (1 Corinthians 7:3-8). There is only one sin that is unforgiveable: blaspheming the Holy Spirit (Matthew 12:31).

I've shocked quite a few people when I say that even God got a divorce. Due to the unfaithfulness of Israel, He served them a document of divorce (Jeremiah 3:8). It was part of His divine plan to look beyond the Jewish nation and include Gentiles in the salvation of humanity. (Gentile refers to anyone not Jewish.) God will forgive and reconcile with His church, which will include the Jewish people who repent and recognize the redeeming work done by His Son Jesus on their behalf. In essence, God divorced and remarried! As controversial as that sounds, it is right there in Scripture. However, keep the balance of the spiritual principle. God still loves and longs after the Jewish nation. He will draw them back to Himself, reuniting with the bride He separated from. That being said, God will not hold man to a greater standard than what He would do Himself; therefore, He allowed divorce for adultery/unfaithfulness. He knows the depth of what this can do to a covenant relationship firsthand.

God does not punish one person for the sins of another (although many people can suffer from the consequences of one person's sin). If a husband divorces his wife and she is not at fault biblically speaking, I believe God would not insist the wife stay single. So if you have been abandoned, rejected, abused, or cheated upon, I believe it's commendable if you can work through the issues, reconcile, and create a healthy marriage. But if you can't, I don't believe God will count it as sin against you if you remarry.

Our God is a God of *reconciliation*. He loves us and reconciles us to Himself so He can heal all our wounds. He is the giver of life and new beginnings. Many Christians offer testimonies of their reconciled marriages, but just as many have testimonies of new beginnings blessed by God. If God doesn't condemn you, you are free to remarry.

Only you and your husband know what happened in your marriage. Did you do all you could? If you weren't capable of doing what it took to salvage the relationship, carry your worries, concerns, and any regrets to the cross of Jesus and leave them there. Ask God to cleanse you, heal you, and give you a new start.

Hopefully, you've learned valuable lessons that God can use as a valuable testimony for Him and that will help you in your next relationship, should you choose to have one.

In this life everyone has baggage. It's the size of the baggage that's important. It is also important to find out if the person you're dating is willing to unpack his issues and sort them out to make room for you and a healthy relationship. Before entering a new relationship, a divorced person needs to take the time to heal from the pain and hurts of his or her previous marriage. To confront the challenges that took place, get real and honest about the part he or she played in the deterioration of the relationship, and evaluate and assimilate the lessons that can be learned. If you've been divorced, make sure you take the necessary time to heal and become whole again. Starting and establishing a healthy new relationship is impossible when you are just a shadow of yourself and your heart is still fragmented. After a marriage ends, the immediate goal is not to find a new partner. No, it should be the restoration of yourself and a healthy rebuilding of your spirit. Then, in your wholeness, should God desire to bless you with another spouse you will be ready.

Dear Michelle,

I am a divorced mother of two small children. I've been on my own now for about two years—my husband left me to be with someone else. Recently I met a really nice man. He is caring, loves my children, and loves me, but I'm getting so much resistance from the people around me.

I feel guilty about finding love again even though my husband left me for another woman! I'm not sure what to do. I feel my children need a father and I need a husband. I need help, to be perfectly honest. Some people believe I shouldn't remarry until my children are old enough to leave home, but I don't honestly think I can raise them on my own. I've been so lonely since my husband left. I feel as if people at church blame me for the divorce so I feel isolated.

What should I do? Should I follow my heart or listen to others?

Sincerely,
In a State of Indecision

Dear Indecision,

Let's break the issues down a little at a time. First, let's deal with your heart recovery. You didn't say how long you'd been married, but it takes time to recover from divorce, especially if it's due to something as traumatic as adultery, abuse, or desertion. Make sure you've taken the time to heal before considering another romantic relationship. This is critical because a desperate woman is a woman who won't make good choices. There is a saying I always like to quote from the book of Proverbs: "A satisfied soul loathes the honeycomb, but to a hungry soul every bitter thing is sweet" (27:7 NKJV). Make sure you are whole enough to recognize a good thing.

Next, check your personal motives for wanting to date and, eventually, remarry. God gives grace for wherever or however He has called us to live. He is a Father to the fatherless and a Husband to the husbandless. He is a present help in time of need. He will send you help for those instances where physical help is needed in the form of great men friends who will pitch in to do the things that need to be done, be mentors for your children, and so forth. So don't let your feelings of inadequacy and need take control and force you to hurry to find a replacement husband, father, and helper.

Yes, the Bible says there is safety in a multitude of counselors. But you must select carefully the people you ask for and receive counsel from. Misery loves company. People who don't understand the love and grace of Jesus might want to keep you as miserable as they are. Use discernment regarding who you talk to. Pray about it, asking God to give you His wisdom for choosing counsel.

There is wisdom in using this new season in your life to focus on your children and raise them with God's help. There are so many things going on in the world that it can be difficult to know who you can trust with your children. The years *go by quickly, and you will never get them back. Make sure your children feel loved, safe, and cared for. Don't use them or their views as a barometer for whether you should consider dating and eventually remarriage. Children are resilient and will adapt well as long as they know they are loved and their needs are met.*

My suggestion for you? Clear your slate with God and take "need" out of the picture. Make sure you are healed and whole. Get objective counsel for where you are as well as whether you should date. If the man in your life is amazing, become best friends instead of rushing romance. Make sure you have a strong conviction and direction from God regarding whether this man is the one for you. Take your time and move forward only after receiving God's direction and peace. He won't lead you wrong.

Take it one day at a time.
Michelle

Keeping It Real

Okay, fact: God hates divorce. Fact: Because we are human and the state of our world, divorce is a reality for many. Fact: There is life and forgiveness and restoration available after divorce. If God does not condemn you, don't let people do it either.

Remember that men are not Band-Aids. I know the popular train of thought is that the best way to get over one man is with another man, but that is just not true. You need to be free emotionally and spiritually—clear and whole—before moving on to another relationship. Otherwise you bring too much baggage into the situation and you might fall into the same type of traps.

So take time for you after a relationship ends. You owe it to yourself to get you back and get centered in who you are in Christ. To take stock of your world and what you would like to do differently next time. Count your blessings where you are, and surround yourself with a strong and warm support system. Celebrate God's faithfulness and love for you. Ask and allow Him to heal your memories and your heart, to erase the negative recordings that threaten to play over and over in your head about your failings and mistakes, and to help you learn from the past and reposition yourself for a successful future. Cling to the lessons not the old emotions.

Walk with God and be open to what He'll bring into your life. He never allows something to be taken away without replacing it with something better. He is able and willing to do that, and He wants to for you.

23

New Beginnings

Whether you've been divorced or simply been through relationship after relationship, if you truly desire to marry at some point you'll have to break the negative cycle. I can tell you from experience that old recordings of negativity can play in your head and sabotage new opportunities for love if you don't find the off switch and then do due diligence in envisioning and positioning yourself for a new beginning and new opportunities to receive the love you long for.

Let me just share a little of my personal story. There was a time in my life when I went through a cycle of disappointments that were similar in nature. It left me with a deep fear of being replaced. I came to the place where I *anticipated* unfaithfulness. I was sure at some point the man in front of me who was claiming how "over the moon" he was about me would have a sudden change of heart and decide he wanted to be with someone else. I was afraid to be happy in a relationship. I was afraid to receive love and afraid to give love because I was no longer secure in the fact that I could have a happy ending. Little did I know I was sabotaging every relationship! Because I didn't feel free to be authentic and open, the men in my life felt the distance and, consequently, never felt safe enough to commit. Many thought I wasn't really interested because I never gave them the clearance to come in close. While I was feeling rejected, they also felt rejected and unsafe. I couldn't see this because I was too busy being in protect mode. Everything was all about me.

I wrapped myself up so well in protectiveness that I also kept myself out of the very relationship I so badly wanted. One day God gave me a vivid illustration. Some people were coming to my house to interview me. They were bringing a camera crew and lots of equipment. I anticipated all these people banging into things and knocking things over. I have a precious collection of art, so I scanned the room for things I should move for protection. There was one statue in particular that I really loved. I took it and moved it far out of harm's way.

The interview went well, and nothing was broken. Later, after everyone had left, I went to retrieve the statue to put it back in its original place. Much to my dismay, I accidentally knocked it over and it broke! At that moment, I heard God say, "Michelle, the very thing you try to protect, you will end up breaking yourself." This was a powerful epiphany for me because that's exactly what I'd been doing in my life. I was protecting myself right out of potentially loving relationships.

I think of the woman at the well who had suffered a series of disappointments (John 4). In fact, she'd had five marriages and was currently joined to a man without the benefit of marriage. She knew the future didn't hold much, and her heart yearned for more. Her life-changing conversation with Jesus brought her to the place of confessing what was no longer working in her life, and she opened her heart to embrace Jesus, who offered her the love she longed for and freedom from her past. But first she had to get real and be honest about where she was. She had to be transparent about what her true issues were and what was on her heart. She had to discern what was truly important, and also see that no human was the key to her lasting happiness. Her heart and mind had to be focused on the only constant source of love and support she would ever have—Jesus.

By looking to Jesus, she placed her trust in Him. And, girl, this is the only way to truly guard your heart. To make Him the primary in your life. By placing your trust in God and not in man, you transfer your heart to a place where it will always be safe. The woman at the well was given confidence and direction when she placed her trust in the Person who would never disappoint her—Jesus.

I'm sure you've heard that "the definition of insanity is doing the same thing over and over yet expecting different results." To get the romantic relationship you want, you will have to ask God to show you the roots of the negative cycles in your life. After that, have some honest discussions with friends and, perhaps, even old boyfriends to uncover your blind spots. Ask them what makes it difficult to be in relationship with you. What do they see in you that might hinder you from finding and keeping a permanent love relationship. Be prepared for the truth, and, yes, it might be painful. But take it in, evaluate it for accuracy, and then decide what you're going to do about it. Growth often comes through difficult circumstance, and risking momentary discomfort so you can grow is worthwhile.

The true power of love is that it enables you to rise above your fears, pride, and insecurities so you can be open to the possibilities.

So how do you guard your heart and stay transparent in love? You allow God to keep your heart while being real about who you are and how you feel with the person you're dating. God will not drop or wound your heart. He will keep it safe. And if it turns out the person you're dating isn't able to handle your authenticity, that's his problem, not yours. At the end of the day you can walk away, if necessary, knowing you were your true self. If the relationship doesn't work out, you won't be questioning your part or wondering what would have happened if you'd kept it real.

The true power of love is that it enables you to rise above your fears, pride, and insecurities so you can be open to the possibilities. Jesus said no one took His life from Him but He laid it down on His own; therefore, He had the power to pick it back up (John 10:17). I believe one of the greatest hurts a person can feel is rejection. It is always easier to handle a breakup if you're the one deciding to cut the cord. When someone says he no longer wants to be with you, it can feel like your very soul is dying. "Why wasn't I enough?" resounds in your mind and plays over and over. And it comes on even more loudly when the next opportunity for love comes, which makes you hesitate. And if you listen to it, you might back out before the relationship has a chance to get started. Or you might repeat the same things that contributed to the difficulties in your previous relationship. The key is to take the time to heal, to allow God to show you your blind spots in relationships and help you work toward greater health. And when you're feeling healthy and whole, and when God brings someone new into your life, then you will be ready to dare to love again.

Dear Michelle,

Why do I always attract the same kind of man? Perhaps I'm not admitting to myself that I'm commitment phobic. There has to be a reason I only attract married men and players who refuse to get married. They're always very interesting men, just not marriage material. I do really want to be married deep in my heart, but obviously I am doing something very wrong.

My male friends say they don't see me being interested in settling down. My sister friends say I don't make room for men in my life. I think I do! So what is the disconnect between what I want and what I am getting? I'm definitely doing something wrong. I think I'm fun and loving. I love men and am not a male basher. I've been told I'm attractive. I don't have trouble attracting men—I just can't get them to commit. All my relationships start off hot and heavy, and somewhere along the way they just *fade to black for no obvious reason. I don't know where I drop the ball along the way, but when I look up the game is over. I'm weary of the cycle. Help!*

Desperate for a Love Coach

Dear Desperate,

I don't usually encourage people to get to a place of desperation, but in your case it's probably a good place to be. That means you're open to change. First of all, we must never discount God's timing when it comes to presenting you to the right man. But let's do some homework while you wait.

You need to check yourself completely because the same things will come up when that right man comes into your life. Your friends have said some pretty interesting things. You need to deal with why men don't believe you want to settle down. Are you sending mixed signals? What is it about your attitude, habits, activities, and things you say that lead them to that conclusion?

Your other friends suggested you don't have room in your life for a man. Is that true? Then perhaps you need to do some spring cleaning—not of your home but in your life and habits to open your world to include more people. Sometimes when we are truly fabulous we can become a bit overwhelmed by our own wonderfulness and exclude others without even knowing it. And sometimes we get into such a happy groove that we don't realize we've left other people out. So check yourself, girlfriend.

Finally, perhaps it's time to change your perceptions and confessions as you move forward. Do you need to reframe what you believe you can receive from God and relationships? To change your self-talk to be more positive? Renew your mind *so that your life can be transformed (Romans 12:2; 2 Corinthians 3:18)? How you talk to yourself reinforces how you act and what you believe (Philippians 4:6-9). So get a new conversation going and let your actions line up with what you want and believe. Do you really desire a husband? Then start thanking God for bringing you the desire of your heart and start preparing for your man's arrival by making the adjustments needed in your mindset and life. Keep in mind that while you wait, it's not just about that man who is coming, it's also about you becoming a better you for Christ, for yourself, and for everyone in your world.*

Here's to a new you and a new day!
Michelle

Keeping It Real

As you claim your new beginning and shatter old relationship cycles, don't just move forward on blind faith. Attach your faith to a promise from God, not the arrival of a man. Here is a good promise to all singles from God. It's found in Isaiah, chapter 62. I'll share a few of these verses from The Message Bible, but you owe it to yourself to read the entire chapter yourself. You won't be disappointed!

First of all, it says God will give you a new name (verse 2). You will no longer be called Rejected or Ruined (4). You will be called Hephzibah (My Delight) and your land Beulah (Married), and your land will be like a wedding celebration (4). (The New International Version says, "your land will be married.")

Next the text says, "I've posted watchmen on your walls, Jerusalem. Day and night they keep at it, praying, calling out, reminding God to remember. They are to give him no peace until he does what he said, until he makes Jerusalem famous as the City of Praise" (6-7). In other words, God will send intercessors into your life to stand on the promises He gives and remind Him of what He's promised to and for you. "God has taken a solemn oath, an oath he means to keep: 'Never again will I open your grain-filled barns to your enemies to loot and eat. Never again will foreigners drink the wine that you worked so hard to produce. No. The farmers who grow the food will eat the food and praise God for it. And those who make the wine will drink the wine in my holy courtyards' " (8-9). Yes, God is saying that He will not allow others to reap what you have sown!

And here is the best part of all! "God has broadcast to all the world: 'Tell daughter Zion, "Look! Your Savior comes, ready to do what he said he'd do, prepared to complete what he promised." Zion will be called new names: Holy People, God-Redeemed, Sought-Out, City-Not-Forsaken!' " (10).

There you have it! The negative cycle is broken. God arises and redeems His promises for you. He gives you a new name as you partner with Him and prepare the road in your life for love to come. So do your homework and stand on His promises! After you have exercised patience and done His will, He promises He will come and not tarry!

24

Ultimate Love

"Then the LORD God formed a man from the dust of the ground and breathed into his nostrils the breath of life, and the man became a living being" (Genesis 2:7). *Wow!* Can you imagine that God kissed man? It was the kiss of life. And from that day forth, we have all craved that eternal kiss. An eternal connection that will not be broken. Yet in our temporal framework, that aspiration for complete oneness goes unrealized.

The earthly relationship of marriage, the connection between a husband and wife, is a mere shadow of our divine connection to God. Marriage is designed to be an illustration of what oneness with God will be like. That is difficult to achieve because we know only in part and are limited by our humanity. Depending on how surrendered we are to God, our relationships may or may not reflect this principle well. The oneness on earth as a couple is a foretaste, a shadow of the wonder and mystery of everlasting love with God the Father and our ultimate bridegroom Jesus. This is why the enemy of our souls attacks marriage so fiercely. He's trying to mar the perfect finish of God's design for us. And this is another reason why it's so important to choose our partners wisely and remain committed to our commitments to God and to our mates.

How can we do that? By not over-spiritualizing ourselves into difficult, natural relationships. Remember, just as the holy trinity is a trifold expression of the personhood of God, we also are triune beings. We consist of a spirit that has a soul living in a physical body. God pays attention to all three parts of us, and we must too. Our choices of mates can't be based on just the fact that we share the same faith. That is a good place to begin, but we'd better have more in common than our faith in God.

As I've noted before, there is a big difference between "being single" and "being alone." As my dear friend Pastor Kofi Banful says, "God did not say it was not good for man to be single. He said it wasn't good to be alone." Let's face it, there are a lot of married people who feel alone. Aloneness was not and is not God's plan or desire for us. He created us for relationship. We were made to be interdependent on one another. In the Garden of Eden, God decided that man needed a helper who was suited to his particular needs. This is why no suitable mate was found from the animals Adam was told to name. It was clear that none were "like kind" with him.

God also commanded man and woman to be fruitful in their union. And this wasn't just about having children. No, it included being fruitful for God's purposes and His kingdom. This is why when a man finds a wife he finds a good thing and obtains favor from the Lord (Proverbs 18:22). It is this favor that opens doors of opportunity. It is this favor that allows man to be successful in what he puts his hand to. God's favor causes man to prosper. That is fruitfulness!

The woman also benefits greatly from this favor granted to man. As both members of this divine team inspire each other, encourage each other to good works, and view the fruit of their labor together, they find a fulfillment in life that can't be achieved by romance and passion alone. It comes out of being partners inspired by the divine and coming into the fullness of their God-given destinies together.

So when a man comes into your life, how do you know he's the one for you? Well, it definitely goes beyond him being cute or setting your heart on fire. It goes down to the core of who you are and what you were designed and called to do. Not everyone will understand you and celebrate and support you as you need to be. The man God brings into your life will. And that works both ways.

As I've said, you need to like, love, and be "in love" with your spouse. I also believe you need to feel assigned to your spouse. Assigned to be the helper who assists him in becoming who God created him to be. There will be a fine balancing act between the two of you regarding all God has deposited within each of you. Your man should "get" you, and you should "get" your man. Marriage isn't a contest. It's a covenant to exercise teamwork in order to obtain victory in your life as one and as individuals. That victory will glorify God and His kingdom.

The Ultimate Bridegroom

Jesus is the ultimate bridegroom, giving us the pattern for what *true* love looks like and what a husband/wife relationship looks like. He patiently waits for His bride while revealing His love for us. He is faithful, gracious, and merciful. He personifies love and loving well. He is slow to anger. He is patient and kind. He forgives us over and over, never giving up on us. In fact, Jesus is the epitome and reflection of the fruit of the Spirit: "love, joy, peace, forbearance, kindness, goodness, faithfulness, gentleness and self-control" (Galatians 5:22-23).

I recall sitting with two friends shortly after they married each other. The husband was telling me why he decided he had to marry his wife. His answer was short and simple, and not framed with fancy accolades. He simply said, "I fell in love with her and had to marry her because she never gave up on me." His wife and I knew this to be true, but it was so profound to hear him say it. That's what true love does. It persists. It keeps on loving; it never gives up. I believe this is what we all seek. That person who loves us so much he refuses to give up on us. He just keeps coming back no matter what. How do we find that person? By being that person ourselves. We will attract people who are like we are or at least who we believe we deserve.

Natasha Bedingfield sings a song that says everyone longs to be loved by someone who knows how to do that without being told. She wonders why she's alone and if there is a soul mate for everyone. I understand that feeling completely. We all long for that lasting human connection. But our greater longing is for an eternal connection, and that can only be achieved with God through Jesus Christ. At the end of the day, no matter how deep, wide, and high your love is with your man, remember there is a section of your heart reserved for God alone. A human will never be able to fill that space. Your happiness depends on knowing your man can't be your source of completion. Only God fills that void. God is your ultimate soul mate. He is the one who breathed into you the breath of life and made you a living creation. His breath, His Spirit, makes you whole. His eternal kiss fills your need for oneness in a love that you can feel and sustains you until God brings your man to you. God is and always has been the ultimate bridegroom, your source of ultimate love. No matter where you are in your journey of love, know that you are never alone. Embrace the one who loves you most. And when your man arrives, love him the way you've been taught to love by the author of love Himself, Jesus Christ.

Dear Michelle,

Not much to say. I just wanted to ask you, "Will I ever find true love?" Sometimes I feel as if I can't breathe, the longing is so intense, and yet there is no one. Why is love so easy for some to find and so difficult for me? People say I'm attractive and fun. I'm successful. If I do say so myself, I would be a prize for the man who got me. I am loving and giving. I so long to have someone to give all my love and support to. Most of all, I long for my own special, intimate friend I can share my life with. It seems a shame to acquire so much and have no one to share it with.

I can't really complain about my life. It is rich, it is full, and yet I feel a void I don't seem to have the grace to fill. Does the longing ever stop? Does the pain go away? Can I *really be sassy, single, and satisfied? You wrote the book, perhaps you have the answer.*

Sincerely,
Single but Not Satisfied

Dear Not Satisfied,

First of all, I feel your pain. I've been there and have visited that space again at various stages in my singleness journey. The reality, my dear sister, is that every day is not the same. I'm sure there are times when you wake up and you are quite happy with your life just the way it is. As you know, "happiness" is a state of mind ruled by circumstances. "Joy" is what God puts inside of us that can't be touched by outward conditions.

Your desire for a mate is a God-given yearning. Desires are all right if you possess them, instead of them possessing you. The enemy tries to pervert everything God has created. The devil will take your longing and try to make it an obsession if you allow him access.

The truth of the matter is that you will have good days and bad days, just as married people have good days and bad days. Part of the dissatisfaction of being single is the fantasy of what you envision marriage will be like. The only way marriage will be fulfilling to you is if you are fulfilled as a single. So while you have the desire to marry, that shouldn't be causing you misery. It should be a healthy desire on your list of other desires that you trust God to bring to pass in the fullness of His timing with the right person who will be a blessing to you.

You've said all the right things. You have a healthy esteem, and your reason for wanting to be married is admirable and right. Therefore, trust God and know He is working on your heart's desires even if you aren't seeing specifics at the moment.

Stand on His promises to you, and step forward in faith. That means you will be preparing to be the best gift God can give to a man. Consider yourself in "Good Thing" rehearsal until God presents you before your audience of one. Hold on a little while longer, girl. Your man is coming. You won't know the day or time, so occupy your life with a smile because you never know who's watching!

Joy be with you.
Michelle

Keeping It Real

The ultimate love you can experience begins by observing the first two commandments as revealed by Jesus. The first is "love the Lord your God with all your heart and with all your soul and with all your mind and with all your strength" (Mark 12:30). The next is to "love your neighbor as yourself" (12:31). Fulfilling these is a full-time job that will take you a lifetime.

Perhaps we spend way too much time looking for someone to love us the way we should love ourselves. Too much time waiting for someone else to complete the picture in our lives when God already has. As we are consumed with love for God, we get a healthy appreciation for whom He created us to be, and we become whole in Him. That is transferred to how we treat others. Everything else becomes a pleasant addition to a cup already running over. As we walk in expectation and a spirit of gratitude, God gives us the grace we need to live joyfully each and every day no matter what our current status. Finding love should never be complicated, just God orchestrated. Trust His timing. Trust the fact that He created you desirable and lovable. Trust that God has the best plans for your life. Trust Him because the best is yet to come.

25

One More Question…

In my travels around the world and from reading what people share on my website (www.michellehammond.com), Facebook page (my friend page is maxed out, but you can like my fan page), and Twitter (@mckinneyhammond), I'm amazed to find that no matter where people are in the world, the issues about affairs of the heart are the same. I can't resist sharing a few more letters I've received that seem to be the icing on the cake of all that we've discussed. I certainly empathize and understand where people are coming from. We all have issues, and we all have needs. Praise God that we all also have access to the ultimate Savior and Bridegroom, Jesus Christ. Hopefully you know by now that you're not alone in wondering about love and men and how they intertwine.

Dear Michelle,

How do I keep my relationship from breaking up even though I've given my man all the space he needs? I love my boyfriend, but yesterday he was confused as to whether to break up with me or if he just needed more space. I tried talking to him, but I was bitter that he was ready to sacrifice the five months we've been dating...

He tells me he has to find himself and make himself happy, and then he will be ready for a serious relationship with me. The problem is he won't give me a time frame of how long the space thing will take. I purposed to stay, but I don't know what to do...I did pray about it and I felt some inner peace, but I am afraid of losing him. He's the only man who has ever made me feel important, and I want this relationship to work. He isn't saved, but I'm determined to help him know Christ. I just don't know how...

Please Help

Dear Please,

First of all, since men aren't possessions, it's impossible to keep one by your own efforts. His desire to be with you keeps him with you. If he's being ambivalent in any way, there is nothing you can do to help him make up his mind. It has to be his choice. To talk him into staying or manipulating him to feel guilty or sorry for you will only prolong your suffering.

If a man says he's not ready for a relationship or that you're too good for him (or other similar statements they use to stay away from committing to a relationship), you need to believe him and act accordingly. If he's saying he has to find himself and doesn't recognize he's standing right there, God needs to help him! He is right about one thing, though. He does need to be happy on his own so that he doesn't hold you responsible for a job you were not created to do. You can't be responsible for his joy level.

Though the heart knows no time parameters, five months is not a long time to be invested in a relationship. Better to find out now that Mr. Man isn't ready for prime-time TV before you get into the storyline too deeply.

The most glaring statement in your letter gave me pause. I'm wondering why we're having this discussion in the first place. You said he is not a Christian. If he's not a Christian and you are, you're fighting a losing battle from the beginning. The majority of your values aren't going to be important to him, and he won't understand the basis for any of them. He might already recognize this and is making excuses to get out of the relationship.

If he is meant to be with you, he will have his experience with Christ without your help. That is a completely personally, one-on-one situation between Christ and this man. You can't make it happen. That's what is called "missionary dating." You've decided you're gonna "save" yourself a husband. Well, it usually doesn't work out well that way and often leads to even more heartbreak. Missionary dating is not the way to go.

Let the guy go, girl, and save yourself the time and the trouble. Release your friend and go your way. If he is the one for you, he'll be back—saved by Jesus and committed to following Him. Then that man will be ready for a relationship with you.

This is where trusting God for the very best comes in. Right now the man in your life is more of a hindrance than a plus. He is blocking the way of real blessing. It's time to move on and make room for what your heart truly desires.

Asking God to bless you with courage,
Michelle

Dear Michelle,

I've been going out with this young man since 2008. He used to drink a lot and was almost always rude to me, *especially when he was in a bad mood. Unfortunately, he was always in a bad mood. He saw the relationship as master/maid then. Because of this, I tried to submit totally to him. I guess it was all a mistake. When I realized it wouldn't help, I decided to back out. By then I had entered into the university. He called me every single day, promising he would change.*

We got back together eventually, but now the story is different. He keeps accusing me, telling me how ungrateful and wicked I am. He keeps suspecting my every move. I have quit the relationship about five times, but I always find myself back in it. He is now seriously trying to persuade me to marry him. He says he is ready to go for counseling on anger management.

The problem is that anytime I tell him I don't want to spend the rest of my life with him, it's as though I feel the pain he goes through. But I am scared of what I may see after marrying him. The truth is, events in this relationship have made me lose interest in relationships period. I have developed this fear toward marriage. What should I do?

Too Afraid to Say "I Do"

Dear Too Afraid,

You should be afraid! Nothing you told me raises any green flags for this relationship. Let's see, consistent bad moods, anger issues, disrespect, condescension, mental and emotional abuse (which, by the way, sounds like it could turn physical any minute), accusations, grudge holding. What is there to love? None of that guy's actions goes with the description of love found in 1 Corinthians, chapter 13.

This man has managed to burden you down with guilt to

make you remain in a relationship you know isn't good for you. C'mon now! You feel his pain every time you choose to walk away? Girlfriend, you can bet you'll feel your own pain if you remain any longer! He has given you a distorted view of love, relationships, and marriage that has nothing to do with God's design.

In this case, you need to get selfish and put yourself first because that is exactly what he is doing. He is controlling you for his own ends. You need to break free, break it off, and move across the country if you need to. Get away from him by any means necessary.

Ask God to heal your heart and your memories and show you the kind of love He wants to shower on you. Please understand that your situation is not healthy. Cut the cord!

You need to take the time to sit and ponder why you feel this man was all you deserved. I suspect there is something in your background that made this situation seem "normal" for you. I highly recommend getting into the Word of God and looking at love from God's perspective. Also discover how precious you are to Him. Since you're so special to God, others had better see your worth and act accordingly. People will treat you as well as you treat yourself. You get to set the standard, and your standard needs to be God's standard. Don't allow anyone to treat you in a way God would object to.

'Nuff said!
Michelle

Dear Michelle,

I love and care for my guy, but he doesn't do the same for me. Can you imagine that we only get to talk when we *have sex? He doesn't call me if I don't call him. I love him very much, and I don't want to lose him. Please help me.*

Feeling the Silence

Dear Silence,

If you could see me right now—my hair is on fire! Did you read your letter before you sent it to me? What are you in love with? You don't have a man or a relationship. You have what the world coins "a booty call"! Now, I don't know if you're a committed Christian, but God's Word is where I take all my rules from. I've said it once, and I'll say it again: Dating is not for mating! Dating is for collecting data. *And that data determine if the man qualifies to be considered for courtship.*

Since you've jumped past all that, I suggest you shut down the relationship and get back to basics. How can you sleep with someone you don't even talk to? What is the basis for your intimacy? What do you love about this man? If he isn't calling you, it's because he doesn't want to call you. I'm guessing he has someone else, and he has categorized you as a bedmate only.

Girl, you can't lose him because you never had him. I can't help you, but you can help yourself. It's time to work on your self-esteem and realize you deserve more than a midnight visit. You deserve to be loved and cherished by someone who sees your value and behaves accordingly. That just makes good sense whether you're a Christian or not.

Sex does not seal the deal, and neither does it get you a man. You have to have much more going on than that to gain a lifetime partner. So call this a lesson learned the hard way and move on. Stop calling him. The man is supposed to pursue you. If you pursue him, he will respond as long as he feels he has nothing better to do. When he finds someone he wants to pursue, he will forget about you. Don't set yourself up for certain disappointment. Like they say, "Drop it like it's hot!" Ask God to help you move on and then make the move to end it. Allow yourself to heal so you will be expectant for the man who will see your precious worth, pursue you, respect you, and treat you with the care God desires for you.

You are a precious child of God!
Michelle

Dear Michelle,

I need help! My guy loves me, but we are not compatible at all. He loves politics and business. I love music. We are always fighting about this. I'm scared to marry him because he may not allow me to do my music and choreography since he's not interested in that. Please help!

Missing the Harmony

Dear Missing the Harmony,

If you're fighting over this now before you get married, what do you think is going to happen after you say "I do"? As a wife you will be called to submit to your husband, and you already don't trust him when it comes to what you love to do. How can two walk together except they agree? I'm not saying you have to be doing what your partner is doing or vice versa, but you must have an appreciation for each other's interests. If he is holding your interest in disdain and doesn't support you enough to let you enjoy it even if he doesn't, this situation will only become more and more uncomfortable.

I think you need to ask yourself what the basis and foundation of your relationship is. What commonalities do you have?

Your faith? Your vision for life? How much do you really share and complement between you? Remember, you're considering this man as a partner for life. You need to have a lot to share to keep the romance, passion, love, friendship, and support strong in your marriage. Being unequally yoked isn't just about faith. It's also about all the other things you will share in life too.

Please take your time to make sure you have enough in common to go the distance in a marriage situation. If you don't, you will end up a lonely married person or, eventually, a divorced person.

Michelle

Dear Auntie Michelle,

I really need your help. I am 24 years old. I've been dating a guy for seven years now. I met this married man who lives in the UK with a white lady who is three years older than he is. He told me the marriage was to get papers to stay in the country.

My concern is that he has four kids with four different women. One lives in Ghana (they divorced 8 years ago) and three (including his current wife) in the UK. He said his marriage was all a big mistake, and that he wants to marry me.

He's in the UK now, but we talk on the phone every day. He treats me very well, and I've fallen in love with him. But I know it isn't right in the sight of God. Please help me with your advice. The funny part is I've fallen out of love with my boyfriend of seven years.

What Should I Do Now

Dear What Should I Do Now,

What you should do now is get your head examined! What are you thinking? The man is married! His track record for constancy is seriously lacking. Four children with four different women!

How do you know if he treats you well? He lives in the UK, and you live in Ghana. When and how did you fall in love with him—on the phone? Really?

My dear sister, it is not funny that you would fall out of love with someone who has been in your life for seven years because you fell in love with someone who is far away and married to someone else. That man in the UK is feeding you a line of baloney. He's as much as confessed he's a user because he married his wife only to get legal papers. Now he's obviously running up her phone bill to call you. She is paying for it, rest assured.

You say this relationship is not right in the sight of God, and you're right. So why are we even having this discussion? What do you expect me to say to you? To ignore God or go ahead and do something God wouldn't agree with? That's not going to happen.

My advice is to acknowledge what you already know to be true. The relationship is not right. The entire situation stinks to high heaven and has red flags all over it. Stop the madness and end this. Don't accept another phone call from this man except to tell him never to call you again. Repent of dishonoring his wife and ask God to forgive you. Then ask God to heal your heart and give you your own loving man for a husband.

As for your old relationship, obviously something was missing. And no man should get that much of your time without a serious commitment on both sides. One thing a woman can't afford to waste is time. The clock is against you if you intend to have a family of your own. A man knows what he wants to do, and if he hasn't closed the deal with you in all this time, it's time you moved on from there as well.

Clear the decks and start anew. This time, walk in God's path and wait for Him to bring you someone with integrity who is free and ready for a real relationship.

Michelle

∽∽∽∽∽

Hello, Michelle,

There is this guy that I'm friends with... We're not best friends. We help each other a lot in ministry. He is the men's department president, and I am a youth group leader. We've known each other for about 16 years, and there has always been an attraction between us. He is very shy, and I have always been very accommodating to him when he reached out for my help.

Lately, I've decided that I'm too accessible to him so I've started to limit how much I help him. I really like him, but we have never gone beyond the occasional flirtation. I've realized that I'm thinking about him a little more than I should.

My question is, was backing off a good move? And how do I get him out of my head if this doesn't result in him pursuing me?

Thank you, Michelle, for letting God use you the way He is and for your help in advance.

Wanting to Make a Good Move

∽∽∽

Dear Good Move,

Indeed, you are right on point. Remember, men will go after what they want. Never settle for dangling carrots. If you make it too easy for them to enjoy all your attention without making a commitment, you can be stuck in neutral territory ad infinitum. If he isn't making a move to make anything happen between you, you need to assume he's content with the way it is and open yourself to other romance possibilities. Only time will tell if the current man will step up to the plate and declare something more. If not, you are free to accept someone in your life who does realize your incredible value and wants to spend his time with you. Kudos to you for taking a step in the right direction.

Michelle

Dear Michelle,

Guday, ma. I have a friend dat we've known each oda for 12 years now. Along de way he fell in luv wit me, but he has a girlfriend already. His action towards me shows he also luvs me too. What do I do?

To Walk Away or Not

Dear Walk,

Indeed, you should run not walk away from this man. You are not an "also ran." It's first place and only first place for you. No woman should ever settle for being less than first in her man's life (after God, of course). If the man has fallen in love with you, he should be honest with his girlfriend, end it, and proceed to pursue you in the way of a man of integrity. If he is in love with you and still keeping his girlfriend, he's having his cake and eating it too! That is totally unacceptable.

Don't get sucked in by empty words that will never be backed up 100 percent because he's with someone else. If there is something he gets from your relationship, he needs room to see what he isn't getting where he is. If you continue to fill in the blanks for his girlfriend, he will never know what is missing and, worse still, won't have to make a choice between the two of you. So by all means and for the sake of guarding your heart, run! Get as far from him as you need to so you can move on, secure your heart, and be available for someone who loves you and you alone in the way that God expects.

Michelle

Hello, Michelle,

I'm 24 years old and a virgin. I've been in two relationships. One was in my teens, which is the one that lasted the longest. I was in this relationship for two years. He accepted the fact that I didn't want to have sex until we married. After I completed senior high school, he started pressuring me for sex, and he finally broke up with me. I've made up my mind not to have sex until after I get married.

I didn't have a relationship with anybody while I was at the university because the men all wanted sex too. The thing is, I do not want to break my virginity until marriage. Some of my friends keep telling me that if I don't give in, I'm not going to get a good guy. They say I might end up with a guy who will only be pretending to love me so he can take advantage of me. And once he does that, he'll leave me, married or not.

I want to know if there is something that I must do that I'm not doing or something that I am not supposed to do that I'm doing. I want to find real love.

I will be very grateful if you reply to my message. I am getting worried because I'm not getting any younger. My *parents also keep asking to meet my boyfriend even though I've told them I don't have one.*

Waiting Until Marriage

Dear Waiting Until Marriage,

Are all of those friends who have told you to have sex to get a good man married? Uh huh, I didn't think so. Sex does not guarantee that you will get and keep a man. I say stick with your principles. At the end of the day when you lay your head down at night, you are at peace with God and with yourself. That's priceless.

Although sex is a wonderful gift, it is only wonderful when it is free of guilt. And it is always best within the confines of a committed marriage relationship because you're honoring God and you're not worrying about your future status with your partner. Abstinence is not something you exercise because of what other people think. Waiting until marriage is God's standard, and following Him is always in your best interest. Your desire to follow Him is also your thank You to Him for all He's done for you. It is part of being a living sacrifice, giving Him your body until He gives you a special man who will be a physical manifestation of His love for you (Romans 12:1). This man God brings into your life will understand your true value and be willing to commit to having all of you by first following God's principles and by giving himself to you.

Hang in there! I know it's difficult to go against the grain of what everyone else is doing and telling you, but that is what separates champions from commoners. As the apostle Paul said, "Do not conform to the pattern of this world, but be transformed by the renewing of your mind. Then you will be able to test and approve what God's will is—his good, pleasing and perfect will" (Romans 12:2). Don't give in to peer pressure. Choose to please God, and you will always be pleasing to the right man for you and pleased with yourself.

Michelle

Dear Michelle,

What does the Bible say about masturbation and oral sex? I don't know who to ask who won't make me feel as if I'm a dirty person. Nobody at church ever talks about these things or when they do they make it sound like they are deep, dark sins.

I've been single a long time, and I want to know if I'm allowed some kind of sexual release. Sometimes I feel as if I'm about to explode! I'm trying to do the right thing and keep myself for marriage, but it's a bit frustrating when I see so many people doing whatever they please and they end up getting married.

I guess I'm wondering if this whole sex and celibacy thing is as deep as we make it out to be. What are your thoughts on this?

Embarrassed to Ask

Dear Embarrassed,

The Bible is glaringly silent on both issues—masturbation and oral sex. It is very specific about sodomy, homosexuality, bestiality, and sex with relatives. But it is silent when it comes to masturbation and oral sex.

The book Song of Songs (also known as Song of Solomon) is very suggestive. Drinking from fountains, entering gardens, and tasting fruit—well, there have been tons of conversations and theological speculations on exactly what all that talk is really about. But the bottom line is that when the Bible is silent on an issue, the answer or resolution of an issue is between you and God. You need to ask Him to give you a personal word on the topic.

To him that knows something is sin, it is sin (Romans 14:14). This means God might say no to one person on an issue and, on the same issue, say yes to another person. Perhaps His actions might depend on each person's tendency to fall into sin in that particular area.

We could have a long discussion on your two issues, to say the least. But the bottom line is nothing is said in God's Word, so it becomes an area you must take up with God on your own. After prayer, wait until the Holy Spirit lets you know the answer.

I think most people are uncomfortable with their sexuality, so this might be why there is such a lack of discussion on sex. But remember, God created sexuality, so sex is good. The devil can only try to pervert what God has already created. Have you noticed that little babies and children touch themselves quite innocently without any notion of right or wrong? Other, usually older, people then tell them it's nasty and unacceptable. Before then, they don't connect the touch to anything except the pleasure it produced in their bodies.

Is sexuality deep? I think it's as deep as we make it. Sexuality is a beautiful gift God gives us. It is to be treasured and not abused. You want to have a healthy respect for passion so that desire won't rule you. So proceed as your conscience before God leads you.

Michelle

Good morning, Ma,

Please, Ma, I need your advice. I am a 27-year-old lady. I reside in Nigeria and am a good reader of your books. There is this guy the Lord has been telling me about. He used to be my neighbor. After we met again, he asked me to be his girl. But he doesn't call me. I do the calling because I know what the Lord is saying concerning him. Ma'am, I am getting tired of him, and I feel like walking away. Please, Ma, I need your advice.

Tired

Dear Tired,

How does this happen? This is the most common deception in Christendom. The Lord tells one person but not the other that so and so is to be his or her mate. When the will of God involves two people, He is well able to communicate His will to both people.

Man was created to be the pursuer. Regardless of what you think the Lord told you, it is important that you stick to God's order for doing things. If this man asked you to be his girl, then where is he and why isn't he calling? No follow-through suggests he wasn't serious. Stop calling him. Take your rightful place as a woman and wait to see if he pursues you.

Jesus, the ultimate Bridegroom, provides the model of what the man is supposed to do. Jesus pursued and wooed us to Himself. He fought for us and died for us. That is the role of the man God puts in your life. If the man you're dating isn't doing any of those things, he is not the one for you.

The man needs to come after you. Stop trying to make God's

Word to you come true through your own human effort. Let go of him. If he is really the man God chose for you, the man will line up with God's will and come after you. And if he doesn't, you need to accept that the word you received was a deception and move on, believing that God has someone else who will step up to the plate and do the right things to win your hand.

Michelle

Hi, Mum,

There's a man of God I love, and I believe he loves me back. He knows about my past, and he has advised me to be a good gal. But now he's asked me for a nude pic of myself. I don't know if he's testing me or what 'cause he says he's not going to talk to me again because I don't want to send it to him. Please advise.

Being Tested?

Dear Being Tested,

Did you say he was a man of God? What man of God or even what decent man would ask a woman he took seriously to send him nude photos? A true man of God and God's man for you will seek to protect everything precious about you. He will protect you and not want to expose you to sin or trouble in any form. This man tells you to be a good girl and then asks you to do something God would not approve of? And now he is emotionally

Love is the most exciting adventure you will experience next to your relationship with God.

blackmailing you because you sense his request is wrong and won't comply? Something is clearly out of whack.

I think you know the answer to this one. This man is not correct. He is a predator who is not surrendered to God. Get away from him quick, fast, and in a hurry. As a matter of fact, if he is in leadership in your church or an organization you participate in, you need to let the pastor or people in charge know. Far too many times these things stay hidden, and the perpetrator continues to wreak havoc with women in the church and elsewhere. And you'd better believe he's doing this to other women or has done this before.

I know you are longing for love and attention, but the wrong type can do great damage to your heart and reputation. Surround yourself with those who are strong enough to pray with you and give you godly advice.

Continue in relationship with this guy? Absolutely not! But I believe you know that already. Allow me to be your confirmation.

Michelle

Hello,

I have a question. What would be your limits with long-distance love relationships? Everything about this person seems so lovely. Thanks again.

Loving Long Distance

Dear Long Distance,

The only thing about long-distance relationships is they can't remain long distance if they are to move forward. At some point, each of you needs to spend time in one another's environment to really get the full picture of who the other person is and how your worlds can blend together. You can talk on the phone until kingdom come and never really know the other person. Too much is hidden by saying or not saying something, whether it's deliberate or not.

The bottom line is that you have to have a plan if you are in a long-distance relationship. Don't allow it to drag on indefinitely. You must be intentional and work toward the goal you both agree on. And make sure that goal has time parameters.

You also must figure out how to be accountable and transparent with one another even at a distance if you're working toward a lasting relationship. Trust becomes an issue that must be addressed. You must agree on how to establish and build trust between you.

Long-distance relationships are becoming more frequent as we travel the world more and commute longer distances. I leave you with this caveat: Try to keep staying long-distance to a minimum time. We were created for relationship, and distance eventually dissipates passion. Any lasting relationship requires nurturing and care, up close and personal.

Michelle

Well, girlfriend, I could share letter after letter, but this book must come to an end sometime. I think we all agree that some aspects of relationships are mysteries, and it takes all types of situations and people for us to learn about the nuances of love and relationships. Hopefully we also choose to learn from the experiences of others as well as our own so we can avoid unnecessary heartbreaks.

Love—especially romantic—is the most exciting adventure you'll experience next to your relationship with God. As with everything else, if you ask for God's guidance and listen to His replies, along with following His divine order and principles, your romantic relationships will be vibrant and full of possibilities.

Remember that dating is your opportunity to gather data. I encourage you to guard your heart but remain open to God's leading. Don't just love much, but choose to love well. Engage your head as well as your heart before committing to a relationship. Don't over-spiritualize by ignoring the practical, including how much you have in common, whether your goals are complementary, and if your lifestyles are compatible. Know your worth and don' t settle for less than what God wants for you. Rein in your unrealistic expectations, and anticipate God's blessings. Give what you want to receive, and trust your love story to God.

Love always,
Michelle

To Contact Michelle,

find her on Facebook or Twitter. To discover more about her ministry and books, log on to

www.MichelleHammond.com

More Encouraging Books by

Michelle McKinney Hammond

101 Ways to Get and Keep His Attention

The DIVA Principle®

How to Avoid the 10 Mistakes Single Women Make

How to Be Found by the Man You've Been Looking For

How to Be Happy Where You Are

How to Get Past Disappointment

How to Get the Best Out of Your Man

The Power of Being a Woman

Right Attitudes for Right Living

A Sassy Girl's Guide to Loving God

Sassy, Single, and Satisfied

Sassy, Single, and Satisfied Devotional

Secrets of an Irresistible Woman

What to Do Until Love Finds You

Why Do I Say "Yes" When I Need to Say "No"?

A Woman's Gotta Do What a Woman's Gotta Do

DVD

How to Get Past Disappointment (180 min.)

How to Get the Best Out of Your Man

Get the Relationship You Dream Of

Do you want more passion? More unity? Want your man to rise to the occasion? Bestselling author and popular speaker Michelle McKinney Hammond shows you how to create a stronger love that will bring you joy and fulfillment, as well as resilience for weathering the challenges every couple encounters. Through a unique look at the life of Esther, you'll gain:

- ideas for inspiring and supporting your man
- a better understanding of how men think and operate
- specifics for helping your partner meet your needs
- innovative ways to bless him...and let him bless you
- suggestions for using these principles to improve other relationships

If you want to build and enhance your love relationship, let your man be your hero. You'll reap the rewards!

Right Attitudes for Right Living

Attitude Is Everything!

Could your life use some positive reinforcement?

Are you looking for daily inspiration for your heart, mind, and spirit?

Do you want guidance in overcoming life's
...to

Bests... m-
mond k... th
underst... er-
spective... ur-
age you

- n
- li
- t
- r